This book gives an excellent insight into the air war over Spain and the German dress rehearsal for World War II.

American Aviation Historical Society

A long overdue tribute to adventurers for whom a foreign civil war promised a new beginning to their lives.

Naval Institute Proceedings

A very fine example of new scholarship on the Spanish Civil War whereby historians can go back and re-examine the motivation and personalities of the volunteers without being rigidly bound into the 1930s frameworks of Left and Right.

Professor Judith Keene
Director of the European Studies Centre
The University of Sydney

This is an eminently readable work....Those with an interest in the WWII period and the subject of aviation biohistory should take a look at this book.

Military and Naval History Journal

Drawing on a wealth of international documentation to shed light on the volunteers' comrades in arms and opponents, Edwards cuts through decades of popular myth to present the often grim realities of their war -- one in which airmen on both sides were learning from scratch the techniques that would be devastatingly commonplace in World War II. What emerges from his study is the portrait of a small, committed and courageous band of unique characters whose deeds, even stripped of mythos, can stand on their own merit.

Aviation History

AIRMEN WITHOUT PORTFOLIO

(Clockwise from top left) Republican airman's wings, emblem of the Italian "Gruppo Cucaracha," emblem of Morato's "La Patrulla Azul" (Blue Patrol), emblem of the German Condor Legion.

AIRMEN WITHOUT PORTFOLIO

U.S. Mercenaries in Civil War Spain

JOHN CARVER EDWARDS

Foreword by
Brigadier General Robert Lee Scott

Airmen Without Portfolio: U.S. Mercenaries in Civil War Spain
by John Carver Edwards

First Edition:
Praeger Publishers
88 Post Road West
Westport, CT 06881
An imprint of Greenwood Publishing Group

Second Edition:
Global Book Publisher
5341 Dorchester Road
North Charleston, SC 29418

ISBN 1-59457-175-9, print ed.

First printing 1997
Second printing 2003

Every reasonable effort has been made to trace the owners of copyright materials in this book, but in some instances this has proven impossible. The author and publisher will be glad to receive information leading to more complete acknowledgements in subsequent printings of the book and in the meantime extend their apologies for any omissions.

TO THE MEMORY OF FRANK GLASGOW TINKER,
U.S. VETERAN AND CASUALTY OF THE SPANISH CIVIL WAR

For most of you, flight is not in you, and never will be in you. Even when you're in aircraft it's not. The great thing about the birds, especially if they're predators, is that anybody who loves them and understands how they operate gets to be like them; his mind, his imagination, can fly with them, and the birds know it.

James Dickey, *To the White Sea*

CONTENTS

Foreword by Brigadier General Robert Lee Scott ix

Preface xi

Acknowledgments xv

Chapter One: The Airmen 1

Chapter Two: Armies of Babel 9

Chapter Three: Polikarpovs Over Spain 23

Chapter Four: La Patrulla Americana 33

Chapter Five: American Paladins in Action 59

Chapter Six: Flying With the Russians 83

Chapter Seven: Mustering Out 99

Chapter Eight: Life and Death After Spain 107

Appendices 117

Selected Bibliography 131

Index 139

Photographic essay follows page 82.

FOREWORD

A salient aspect of the Spanish Civil War was the extent of the participation of foreign troops to a degree as then unparalleled in any domestic conflict. The ideologically polarized contestants who were vying for control in Spain prompted sympathetic world governments on the far right and left to speculate on what the outcome of the Spanish struggle would mean for their own national and geopolitical interests. The prospect of a totally communist or purely fascist regime in Spain horrified the leaders of the Great Powers (East and West) and destroyed any chance of a peaceful alternative to civil war.

From the beginning, appeals for assistance from both combatants were answered, as Mussolini and Hitler on the one hand and Russia on the other committed men and equipment. Tragically, both sides assumed that the deployment of substantial military power would hasten victory.

Far less conspicuous in their support of the Republican cause were the members of the Non-Intervention Committee, or NIC—Great Britain, France, Yugoslavia, Czechoslovakia, and Poland—countries that had declared their neutrality, but nevertheless continued to dispatch covert arms shipments and proxies to the Loyalist government. As the aid was sent in a clandestine way and through too few channels, the amount of material support was always meager.

Influenced by isolationist sentiment and appeasement-minded politicians, the U.S. government also embargoed aid to the Spanish belligerents, a policy ostensibly meant to de-escalate the war but whose enforcement undermined the Republic. While Nazi Germany and fascist Italy supplied Franco with troops and equipment, the U.S. ban only prevented arms from reaching the Loyalists. Adding insult to injury, several American corporations actually aided the Nationalist cause with trucks and gasoline.

Well documented is the record of those Americans who served with the Abraham Lincoln and George Washington battalions, volunteers who fought alongside the British, Irish, Canadian, and other nationals comprising the Fifteenth International Brigade. Historical notice, too, has been made of the brave U.S. men and women who worked with the American Medical Bureau as nurses, doctors, ambulance drivers, and medical technicians.

Less well known, however, are the exploits of those American airmen who flew for the Spanish Republican Air Force against the best that Franco, Mussolini, and Hitler could send. Perhaps this oversight is due to their limited numbers, or perhaps the fact that these aviators accepted mercenary wages for their services. It is regrettably true that a few of these pilots were unprepared for duty or acted unprofessionally while overseas, but the majority of these men acquitted themselves with distinction, and a select few outclassed their fascist adversaries in fighter aircraft over Spain.

This book is the story of U.S. air involvement during Spain's civil war, pure and simple, a stark look at a handful of adrift and financially strapped American flyers who for a time found a new direction and a worthwhile cause to serve in another country's fratricidal war. Far ahead of American public opinion back home, these flyers were painfully aware of the menace of fascism during the early months of 1937, and they understood that the wolf at Republican Spain's door would eventually beset their own hearthand home.

This work is wonderful history and revolves around fighter pilots; I know we're all peculiar, but there never has been a more interesting profession. The history of World War II is incomplete without reading this work.

Robert Lee Scott
Brigadier General, USAF (retired)
Fighter Pilot
Author: *God Is My Co-Pilot*
Museum of Aviation
Warner Robins, GA

PREFACE

The word mercenary conjures up in the popular imagination the timeless picture of amoral and apolitical adventurers who live to fight and love to kill. One might correctly agree that this breed of soldier has plied his trade since the dawn of human history. It came as no surprise to anyone, therefore, that with the onset of manned flight and the development of aerial combat during World War I that many such soldiers of fortune would emerge both from the ranks of unemployed aviators and from America's next generation of air-minded youth, the latter inspired by wild and wonderful stories from the Great War.

There had been random postings for these flyers-for-hire before, during, and after the war: serving for and against the revolutionary armies in 1913-14 Mexico, hiring out as pilots to the Lafayette Escadrille, bombing and strafing Berber tribesmen on the Moroccan front, fighting for the White Russian and Polish armies against the Bolsheviks, and also making cameo appearances in Paraguay's civil war and in the Greco-Turkey Balkan conflict of 1922. When international assignments became scarce, these roustabout aviators fell back on bootlegging as stopgap employment.

Fellows of this stripe regarded the Spanish Civil War as an unparalleled opportunity for fame, fortune, and adventure. It offered the prospect of conflict on a grand scale and the coffers of the Spanish Republic thrown open to reward deserving airmen fighting on its behalf. There were Popular Front recruiters in the United States and elsewhere in the world to paint these rosy pictures for prospective candidates. With a few shining exceptions, most of these men expressed no ideological interest in the civil war or repugnance to fascism in general, although the butchery perpetrated by Mussolini's air force in Ethiopia struck them as excessive and cowardly.

All of these volunteers expected to fly combat and to be well compensated for their services. The marginal pilots were destined to be disappointed in their flying appointments and reduced pay; a few were sent back home as either personally or professionally unacceptable, while more accomplished aviators accepted transport and reconnaissance duty. Only a handful of the U.S. arrivals would be assigned to combat roles; of this select number, Frank G. Tinker stood apart as one of the Republic's premier fighter pilots.

For their service to the Loyalist cause, members of this elite circle endured revilement back home in the press and on Capitol Hill; personal aggravation from the Republic's bureaucratic war machine and repressive political system; poor medical care and irregular paydays; and the arduous task of waging war alongside other international and native pilots involving polyglot fighting situations. In addition to these challenges, there was always the possibility of death at the hands of a resourceful enemy. Frank Tinker himself would ultimately forfeit his life not in some hotly contested dogfight in Spain, but rather stateside in a heroic but losing struggle with his own government. Given Washington's foreign policy of shameful appeasement in the face of mounting Axis adventurism and its punishment of him for his defiance of so obvious an evil, he could no longer reconcile himself to the land he once loved. As warrior and prophet, he was a man well ahead of his time.

This work offers the reader not only a concise history of the American volunteers' involvement in the Spanish Civil War, but also affords a sense of their burgeoning allegiance to the Republican cause over time. The flavor of the air war is captured in the surreal juxtaposition of international pilots subjected to the tedium of base life and to life-and-death combat situations on a daily basis. From the destructive ratcheting effect of this existence, one comes to a fuller appreciation of the harm done to the flyer's physical and emotional well-being over the course of multiple air campaigns. The accumulated memoirs of the U.S. airmen and those with whom they fought effectively illuminate the contributions of these shadowy mercenaries and, at the same time, tend to humanize a formidable enemy, for surely one side cannot be portrayed without the other.

The following account is not a comprehensive military history of Spain's civil war. The geographical areas and sectors of air operations examined in this study are limited to the duty locations of the volunteers themselves. The ensuing chronicle will also suggest that the mere act of waging war for profit and action does not preclude the possibility of a soldier's commitment to a people, a government, or an ideological cause. The term mercenary as it appears in this work does not address the questions of character, ethical conduct, or one's capacity for moral outrage and political conviction; rather, the term is used to define a pilot's condition of employment and nothing more. From this perspective, it is the author's belief that the basic humanity of each volunteer can be more fully appreciated.

ACKNOWLEDGMENTS

I would like to thank Brigadier General Robert Lee Scott, Jr., of the Museum of Aviation at Robins Air Force Base, Warner Robins, Georgia, for taking the time to write the Foreword to this history of U.S. flyer involvement in the Spanish Civil War.

I am also indebted to the University of Georgia Libraries and the University of Georgia Research Foundation for making available to me the time and financial resources necessary for the completion of this book.

A special thanks goes to Judith Task Quinlan and my daughter, Leigh Carver Edwards, who believed in this story and hastened its telling in so many ways.

A final salute to Senior Editor Dan Eades of the Greenwood Publishing Group. His contributions to this volume are greatly appreciated.

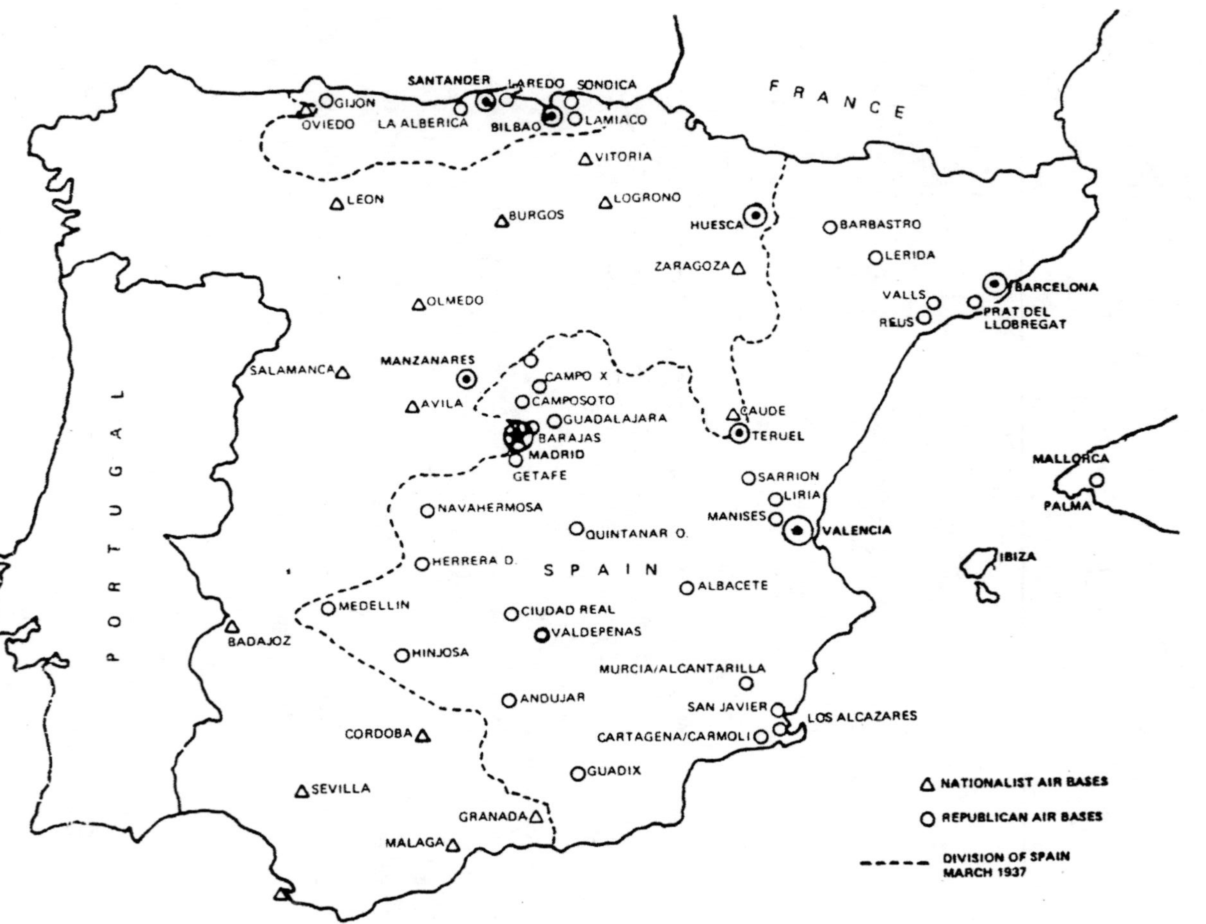

Map of Spain showing the various Republican and Nationalist airbases during the war. *Allan Herr.*

1

THE AIRMEN

Scratch it on a cake of ice and stick it in the oven.

Bert Acosta to Accommodating Bartenders
Thomas Foxworth, *Bertram B. Acosta*

It was April 9, 1937. Scarcely above the shell-pocked buildings of Madrid, a squadron of Russian-built I-15 biplanes roared overhead, having just attacked Nationalist trenches in the Casa de Campo, a suburb across the Manzanares River from Spain's capital. The deafening clatter of the fighters' engines reverberated within the municipal canyons below and mixed with the hysterical screams of 600,000 approving Madrileños to create an awful din. Shouts of "La Gloriosa" rang out again and again from within their ranks. The people of this garrison metropolis had a right to celebrate, to consign the "criminal facciosis" to hell, and to praise their aerial deliverers, after having endured months of siege. It would be different now with Russian and mercenary volunteers to help Spanish Loyalist pilots protect Madrid from enemy bombers and a Rebel army that menaced its existence as the symbol of democratic Spain.

Standing amidst flying shrapnel and ricocheting bullets, the animated multitude pointed upward as if to touch lovingly the little forest green-and-gray Polikarpovs proudly bearing red Republican stripes. As the stubby pursuits flew over the city, one particularly dominant I-15 bearing the fuselage code CA-56 caught the attention of the gallery. Inside its cockpit, Frank Glasgow Tinker was at the controls. Looking down at the throng, the best mercenary combat pilot in the Spanish Civil War could not believe his eyes: "What with machine guns hammering away . . . the shrieking and whining of wind through struts and flying wires . . . the outraged roars of motors protesting at the bottoms of dives . . . the sharp, hollow-sounding explosions of antiaircraft shells. . . . Of course, we couldn't hear the cheering . . . but we could almost feel the waves of acclamation emanating from them." For Tinker, at this moment, no coin of the realm could have compensated him as much as this spectacular outpouring of gratitude, respect, and affection.

Born in Kaplan, Louisiana on July 14, 1909, the son of Frank Glasgow and Effie Tinker, young Frank's family moved to DeWitt, Arkansas where the boy migrated through his adolescence and high school in perfectly normal fashion. At seventeen, he enlisted in the Navy in hopes of winning an appointment to the Naval Academy, a dream realized three years later. Tinker graduated with the Class of '33 earning a B.S. degree, but because he placed in the lower half of his class—and due to the Great Depression—the midshipman did not receive a commission right away. After graduation, Tinker and a host of classmates enlisted in the Army Air Corps as flying cadets and were assigned to Randolph Field, Texas, where they underwent flight training and where Frank survived the instructor's axe.

The Navy received permission to commission the second half of '33 in the spring of 1934, and Tinker submitted himself to flight instruction once again—"the Navy way." While stationed at Pensacola, Florida, members of his squadron purchased special identification bracelets, all of which were silver except one numbered thirteen. It was of gold, and Tinker drew it. When his plane crashed during the training maneuvers of the Pacific Fleet in May 1935, he blamed the bracelet. With Pensacola behind him, Tinker drew assignment on the new cruiser *San Francisco* piloting reconnaissance floatplanes from the ship's catapults. Try as he might, and despite his flying acumen, the young ensign would last only six months in the service. Tinker had worn the maverick's mantle since his Academy days, and although he seldom fomented trouble—being a hail-fellow-well-met—he also enjoyed the reputation of never giving an inch when it came his way. Long Beach, California was the scene of his first brawl, which ended in a court-martial; and another scrape in Honolulu several months later made additional disciplinary action inevitable. Navy brass opted to dissolve his commission, and within a week this troublemaker had traded a berth on the *San Francisco* for one on a Standard Oil tanker. For the next year, 3rd mate Tinker's ship plied the coastwise oil routes. Shipboard tedium and predictable wages exhausted the seaman's patience, however, and when civil war erupted in Spain, Tinker saw his chance.

He cared little for Italian fascism after Benito Mussolini's adventures in Ethiopia, attempting to volunteer to fly for the Addis Ababa government, only to learn that Emperor Haile Selassie had neither recruiters for an air force nor an air force itself. From DeWitt, Tinker wrote identical letters to the Spanish ambassador in Washington, the Spanish consul-general in New York City, and the Spanish ambassador in Mexico City, sending along his résumé. The ambassador in Washington wrote that Madrid required no pilots. From New York City, the consul-general placed the American on a polite hold. But the Spanish ambassador to Mexico wired Tinker to come immediately and sign a contract. The Republican cause agreed to pay him \$1,500 a month with a bonus of \$1,000 for every Nationalist plane shot down. It did not take Frank long to realize that sixty days of flying for his new employers would pay him more than a Navy ensign could possibly earn in a year! The agreement rechristened the Arkansas recruit as Francisco Gomez Trejo, of Oleiros province of La Coruña, and granted him a sealed envelope containing train fare to New York City and traveling expenses. Once at his destination, the Spanish consul-general's office interrogated Tinker closely before sending him to an American lawyer for final instructions. The attorney gave him a ticket on the *Normandie* for Le Havre, France the next day, together with a Spanish passport and more expense money. As a final precaution, the counselor made Tinker sign his new Spanish name twenty times, thereby reducing the chances of his scribbling his old moniker on the passenger list at the pier.

French officials in Le Havre, although indifferent to this strange Spaniard's inability to speak his own language, nevertheless chastised him for entering their country with a counterfeit passport. Republican agents met him in Paris and packed Tinker aboard a train bound for the Spanish border. Aboard, he fell into company with the Catalonian foreign minister and the agricultural minister, who provided him safe passage to Port Bou, where he and his Loyalist chaperons changed trains for Barcelona. Subjected to his first air raid in that city, Frank purchased fare for Valencia, where he reported to the Air Ministry the next day. Despite the Ministry's attempt to place him as a regular officer in the Spanish air force at an enormous reduction in salary, Tinker demanded his mercenary's wages and won. First assigned to Los Alcazares airfield, he learned that fellow American pilots were stationed at nearby San Javier, so he proceeded there. Tinker and Harold Evans Dahl, alias Hernando Diaz Evans, soon became fast friends.

FELLOW DECEMBER VOLUNTEERS

After less than three years as a second lieutenant in the Army Air Corps, Harold E. "Whitey" Dahl lost his commission in February 1936 as a result of compulsive gambling and a civil court conviction. From a technical perspective, it proved to be a loss for the Army as the maverick Dahl was a natural-born flyer. With his training behind him at Randolph and Kelly Fields during his military stint, he had flown the first run of army-carried mail into Atlanta, Georgia in the midst of the airmail emergency of 1934. Back in civilian life, Dahl worked as a freelance pilot for a time, experienced a nasty scrape with some Los Angeles gamblers, and fled to Mexico City. There he flew airships between the capital and Vera Cruz, solicited charter flights on the side, and even ferried aircraft to Vera Cruz for shipment to the Spanish Republicans. During this period, he broke bread with agents of the Loyalist Air Ministry in Spain. This twenty-eight-year-old Champaign, Illinois native cared nothing about Spanish politics, but he understood that Iberian women were lookers. He contracted to fly for the Republic on one condition: that the Valencia government include a girlfriend in his travel allowance.

Five years Dahl's senior, Edith Rogers hailed from Seattle, Washington. Beginning her career in the 1920s as an entertainer, when she dropped her family name of Kaye for Rogers, this Swedish-American bombshell was known for her musical virtuosity. An accomplished violinist, her main act was pretending to be otherwise. Rogers had been a showgirl in Earl Carroll's *Vanities* and a vocalist and comedienne with Rudy Vallee, Martha Raye, and Joe E. Lewis.

The Spanish government met Dahl's condition and assured him that he was only to act as an instructor of aviation in Spain. Whitey planned to travel to New York City and meet the other December volunteers about to board the liner *Normandie* for France. When he crossed into Texas, however, the San Antonio police apprehended him on the Los Angeles charge. A weekend in the calaboose allowed him the time to retain a lawyer and successfully present his case. Back on the street, Dahl forfeited his trip to New York City and returned to Mexico. To celebrate their good fortune, Whitey and Edith arranged for a modest Mexican civil marriage—one of dubious legal standing in the United States. The couple could not obtain passports to civil war Spain; instead, they were given papers identifying them as Mr. and Mrs. Hernandez Diaz Evans. The newlyweds sailed from Vera Cruz on December 8 aboard the French liner *Mexique* and docked at St. Nazaire on December 21; five days later they crossed into Spain at Port Bou.

To be sure, Whitey had outworn his welcome in the United States. The War Department got wind of his intentions and alerted the State Department, and by then he had become the *bête noire* of both federal agencies. Dahl's shenanigans in America and abroad would have lasting repercussions for his wartime comrades in years to come.

Boredom plagued Edith Dahl from the start, so she took Whitey's earnings and decamped for Cannes on the French Riviera, residing at the Hotel Miramar. Whenever possible, Dahl inveigled a week's leave and joined his lady on the Côte d'Azur; and although his person could usually be found strapped inside a Chato fighter, his mind would be elsewhere—a dangerous preoccupation indeed!

BELL, DICKINSON, AND GOMEZ

Aside from Whitey Dahl, the other December volunteers included old-timers Orrin Dwight Bell and Derek Dickinson, both of whom were at least forty, and Miguel García Granados, whose true identity was Colonel Manuel García Gomez, a former Guatemalan air force commander who served as interpreter for the Americans.

As a seventeen-year-old lad from New York City attending Vitoria University in Toronto, Canada, Bell had dropped out of school and joined the British Royal Flying Corps. Once in England, he went into training as a military pilot at Cromwell and Killingholme. Lieutenant Bell pronounced it a lovely war, and he claimed six enemy planes and a German Zeppelin in the bargain: "The girls loved a uniform, the drinking was pleasant, and you had just enough action . . . to make life interesting." At thirty-eight, Bell tried to manage a floating seaplane base on the Jersey side of the Hudson River and lost the whole business in the Great Depression. With $50,000 blown to the wind, he saw the Spanish embroglio as a godsend.

Colonel Gomez, alias Granados, left a wife and four children in Mexico City; he even resigned his commission in Guatemala's air force to enlist. It seemed a shame to refer to him as a mercenary as his dedication to the Republic was beyond question. Whenever Gomez talked about the cause of liberty, his dark eyes blazed and his hatred of fascism amounted to an obsession.

ALLISON, KOCH, AND BAUMLER

Tinker learned that three additional December arrivals had preceded him on the *Normandie*–Jim Allison, Charlie Koch, and Albert J. (Ajax) Baumler–and that the threesome had been sent to combat pilot school in Valencia for certification. Unbeknownst to the others, only Tinker and Dahl had signed contracts designating them as fighter pilots, although the Arkansan underwent several flight checks at Los Alcazares and San Javier.

Tinker understood that Jim "Tex" Allison left a wife behind in Texas in the family way. When asked why he was in Spain, aside from the money, this ex–U.S. Navy pilot from Dallas would always say: "Right's right, and I shore aim to put my oar in and see that the right side wins." Al Baumler failed his U.S. Army Air Corps training for taking off in a twin-engine trainer that had nearly empty fuel tanks. He emergency landed his plane with minimal damage, but was nevertheless washed out for failure to demonstrate proper flying proficiency–and apparently because he showed little aptitude as a potential combat pilot. This twenty-two-year-old flyer hailed from Trenton, New Jersey.

At forty-two, Charlie Koch was perhaps the oldest U.S. volunteer to come to Spain. He learned flying while a student at the University of Georgia; his instructor, Howard Rinehart, had flown as a pioneer mercenary with Pancho Villa's pathetic air force during the Mexican Revolution of 1914. Abandoning college in 1917 to join England's Royal Flying Corps, he contracted influenza and missed combat in France, serving out the war as a flight instructor. From war's end until 1936, Koch worked as an aeronautical engineer for Chance-Vought, Keystone Aircraft, Curtiss-Wright, Rose Aviation, Burnelli Aircraft, and the Seversky Aircraft Corporation.

In late November 1936, his old World War I flying comrade Fred I. Lord, wrote him that money and adventure awaited in Spain. Koch took the bait partly because he missed combat duty in 1917. He left his last employer without notice and no forwarding address. On January 7, 1937, Koch graduated as a Piloto DeCaza (Fighter Pilot) and received orders, along with Tinker and Dahl, to report to a Breguet 19 bomber squadron at Manises Airfield. The three U.S. pilots flew with Britishers Papps, Fairhead, Loverseed, and an unidentified Irishman. The squadron leader, English-speaking Austrian volunteer Walter Kantz, hoped the unit would garner as much public attention as André Malraux's contemporary Escadre España. Tinker served as the squadron's chief navigator. Aside from coastal patrol, sporadic bombing sorties were flown for periods lasting three hours. Ancient French Nieuport 52 fighters accompanied the Breguets occasionally.

Tinker hated flying the antiquated Breguet bombers: huge, lumbering, single-engine, 1920s biplanes. During his debut aloft in this crate, he discovered that packs of propaganda leaflets had been left in the floor of his open cockpit from a previous sortie, and as he gained airspeed the tracts began flying up and plastering him in the face, obscuring his vision and nearly forcing him to crash. Subsequent instruction in formation flying almost proved as disastrous when several ill-trained English pilots nearly rammed his Breguet in flight. Once on combat patrol, Tinker's bomber formation suffered from poor navigation, missed targets, and panicky escort pilots who abandoned the slow Breguets at the sight of Italian pursuits.

On January 12 the so-called International squadron received orders to bombard Rebel positions near Teruel, a city 75 miles northwest of Valencia. When three enemy fighters attacked the bombers, escorting Nieuports again fled. A few Breguets turned tail as well, although others, including Tinker and Koch, stayed the course. Back at base, the lead Breguet cartwheeled on landing; its luck held, however, as the bomb load failed to explode. That evening, during dinner at a Valencia restaurant, members of the squadron came under fire from an Insurgent cruiser laying offshore.

Soon after, the Americans left the Breguet group as they could not get along with their English cousins; all agreed, however, as to their low opinion of the Breguets and Nieuport fighters, the officers, and the inability to collect their pay.

2

ARMIES OF BABEL

The fact that we were fighting for a people other than our own, carrying out sorties deep into enemy territory, and the responsibility for irreplaceable, highly qualified personnel, all this inhibited the keenness and natural élan of the German fighter pilot. He could only operate all-out when his own force's aircraft were in danger.

Hauptmann Günter Lützow
Condor Legion

All in all, I believe I am safe in stating that the Spanish Government treated us much better than our own Government would have done.

Second Lieutenant Frank Tinker

The Russian aircraft are far and away superior in their flight characteristics, the Italians have far better machines—and what does Berlin do? It orders that the HE 51 is better than the Russian aircraft! The bluffing of the past three years must finally stop! What keeps us here is definitely not ideals, rather our youthful enthusiasm, lust for adventure and the 1,200 Marks combat pay.

Hauptmann Harro Harder
Condor Legion/December 1936

At the moment Tinker resolved to seek his fortune in civil war Spain, the horrendous six-month-old fratricidal conflict had seemingly gone on forever. Battles had been won and lost there; military and political reputations had been made and broken there. Truth, too, fell victim to partisan rhetoric and blatant propaganda appeals from the Popular Front government and the Nationalists. The outcome of the Spanish Civil War did not kill democracy in that country; rather, representative government had been compromised for some time before a military cabal sparked a rebellion in Morocco. Advocates of the Republican government could not dismiss the political repression, summary executions, destruction of church property, the desecration of its icons, and the outright murder of clergy, all part and parcel of the regime. The civil war itself only served to focus and energize antidemocratic tendencies abiding at both poles of the political spectrum in the mushrooming leftist and anticlerical tide behind the Republic and the broadening rightist supporters of Francisco Franco.

Since 1931, Spain had been a Republic; and during the ensuing two years, the first elected government formulated radical changes aimed at bringing the nation into a modern world. There were attempts to curb the power of the Catholic Church, such as dissolving the Jesuit Order, the closing of parochial schools, and the abolition of state support for the clergy. A Catalonian autonomy bill was passed in the Cortes as an early gesture to Basque and Catalonian separatists. Agrarian legislation was also enacted aimed at ameliorating the plight of Spain's peasant class. These liberal reforms were challenged by the landed gentry, the Catholic Church, the military establishment of the Spanish armed forces, financiers and industrialists, and a fascist party. A more moderate Popular Front coalition came under fire from its extreme left-wing members who attempted to quicken the movement's political pace with bloody demonstrations, church arson, and terror bombings. As public unrest grew, a conservative government under Alejandro Lerroux (1933) began to dismantle the reforms previously enacted. The result was a revolt in the Asturias which left 4,000 dead in its wake and 30,000 in jail as well as a failed secession attempt by the Catalonians, who together with the Basques had traditionally protested for independence. In due course, Lerroux's government collapsed, the victim of a financial scandal, and a leftist coalition came to power in March 1936. As a signal to potential political troublemakers, civilian and military, the new government dispatched designated military officers to distant garrisons. These men immediately began to devise a plan to end the Republic and replace it with a military junta. The generals garnered the backing of the monarchists with an offer to reinstate the king and also gained the support of the fascist Falange to whom they promised power.

In April 1936 the newly elected Popular Front government appointed General Núñez de Prado as Director General de Aeronáutica. Persuaded that a military coup was imminent, Núñez de Prado concentrated all the best Government operational aircraft on the aerodromes around Madrid. Targeted planes were recalled from air units at León and Longroño to nearby Getafe, and those planes slated for Africa were kept at Cuatro Vientos.

CIVIL WAR

The rebellion commenced during the night of July 17–18, 1936, with a revolt in Spanish Morocco of the Army of Africa, a colonial force of Foreign Legionnaires and Moorish Regulares, led by veteran officers of the Moroccan War of 1909–26. The Insurgents seized the colony within hours, and the following day General Franco flew there from the Canary Islands to assume command. Simultaneously, similar uprisings flared up all over Spain, beginning on July 18, and within three days' time General Emilio Mola had claimed most of northern Spain except Catalonia and a corridor along the Cantabrian and Biscay coasts. These territories encompassed the Asturias and three of the Basque provinces. Although Catholic and conservative, the Basques had aligned with the Republic in exchange for a promise of independence.

The Nationalist revolt failed in Madrid, in all the Mediterranean port cities from Barcelona to Málaga, and in the majority of central and southern Spain. Franco's lieutenants did capture the southwest corner of Andalusia, however, and this prize included the aerodrome and depot at Tablada, Seville. The crews of Republican warships and other vessels in the Mediterranean refused the direct orders of their officers to participate in the rebellion. These steadfast seamen either killed or incarcerated their superiors and steamed into the Straits of Gibraltar to interdict the mutinous Army of Africa in Spanish Morocco from crossing to the mainland. The possibility of a massive airlift was broached, and, on July 19 and 23, the Rebel chieftains dispatched representatives to Rome and Berlin with requests for troop transport and fighter aircraft. Meantime, Nationalist soldiers were sent to Seville to strengthen General Queipo de Llano's slim control of that city and to fashion a bridgehead from which to marshal African army troops when the Italian and German cargo planes arrived.

FRANCE LENDS SUPPORT

In Madrid the Loyalist government forwarded a request to Premier Léon Blum of France, who headed a Popular Front phalanx similar to the government in Spain. Blum summoned an extraordinary session of his government on the afternoon of July 25. Together with the Council, he met with Fernando de los Ríos. By that evening, the Spanish ambassador had agreed to the resolution "not to hand anything over from one government to the other, but to give private industry special authorisation to supply and distribute the armaments we acquire." This succinct position statement formed the text of a letter, communicated by Fernando de los Ríos to the Madrid government, in which he declared that the aircraft sought would be brought out of France before the 27th.

Aviation minister Pierre Cot quietly provided for the transfer of Potez 540 bombers and Dewoitine 372 fighters from French stockpiles to the Republican Air Force, together with such other concessions as allowing Loyalist fighters to refuel in France during cross-country flights from Catalonia to the Basque Atlantic coast, permission for Government pilots to train at French flight schools featuring French instructors, planes, and governmental facilities, and the creation of Air Pyrenées, a government-backed airline to support the Republican cause. Blum continued to toy with the idea of direct aid to Spain, but the premier surrendered this notion when the British government refused his invitation to recall Parliament to discuss assistance to the Loyalists. As soon as it was announced that the last thirteen Dewoitine fighters and six Potez 54 bombers were en route to Barcelona, Blum's cabinet, on August 8, elected to deploy a plan of Non-Intervention.

A month later all the European capitals had either penned the Non-Intervention Agreement or imposed embargoes of their own. A Non-Intervention Committee was created in London with delegates from all the signatory countries to monitor compliance.

ANDRÉ MALRAUX INTERVENES

Within a week following the outbreak of the Spanish Civil War, the magnetic French writer and archeologist André Malraux addressed a throng of Parisians in the Palais du Sport: "Who will come with me to Spain to start a Loyalist air force?" Nearly one hundred Frenchmen stepped forward, and Malraux chose the best of them: idealists who wanted to stop fascism in Iberia; long-in-the-tooth World War I combat airmen who relished the hunt; and an assortment of neurotics addicted to adventure. Malraux offered these volunteers a renewable, monthly contract, based on a salary of 50,000 pesetas and life insurance of 500,000 pesetas.

Once in Spain, Malraux fixed machine guns in the windows of all transport planes available. In a week's time, his squadron was fighting with German and Italian volunteers as well as Spanish Nationalist pilots. From the beginning of August, the Escadre España undertook operations over the Madrid Sierra, using Barajas airport as its base. The unit enjoyed Dewoitine fighter cover from Barajas and Getafe aerodromes, these escorts led by Malraux's fellow countryman Abel Guídes.

For the balance of 1936, the group fought on many fronts, bombing the Alcázar of Toledo, the approaches to Madrid, and wherever there were targets of opportunity. The attrition rate on men and machines was terrible, yet Malraux always managed to scrounge additional planes from France, and his airmen included Germans, Americans, Italians, Frenchmen, White Russians, and one Algerian. He made monthly trips to Paris to meet with airplane manufacturers and officials of the Air Ministry, pleading for assistance. Back in Spain, Malraux fronted for his group, protected the Escadre España from the Loyalist government and meddling Communist commissars, and insured its integrity.

By winter the Escadre España at Albacete represented no more than five or six worn-out aircraft. Only the growing tide of Russian pursuits and bombers offered a glimmer of hope to the Republican cause. In late November 1936, Malraux's chief lieutenant, Julien Segnaire, quietly arranged with the Spanish Air Ministry to rename the Escadre España the Escadre André Malraux. During December the trickle of antiquated aircraft from France ceased, and French authorities even impounded U.S. planes purchased by the Republic and destined for Loyalist aerodromes.

The Frenchman's tour of duty was at an end. He had been twice wounded on 65 sorties. Concluding last-minute business arrangements for his squadron several weeks into December, Malraux flew to Paris. In January 1937 the remnants of the Escadre participated in the Málaga campaign, after which it was moved to Señera, Valencia, where it stayed until disbandment in early summer of 1937. Malraux returned only to make his film *Sierra de Teruel* in 1937 and 1938.

HITLER AND MUSSOLINI JOIN THE FIGHT

Germany and Italy sent aircraft to Franco in August—more machines than he had requested—replete with aircrews, armaments, maintenance support, and even anti-aircraft batteries to protect Rebel air bases: six Heinkel He 51s and twelve Fiat CR 32s, nine Savoia-Marchetti (SM) S. 81 bombers and twenty Junkers Ju 52/3m bomber-transports to Tetuán or Cádiz; and twelve planes to Mallorca—three SM. S. 55Xs, three Fiat CR 32s, three Macchi M. 41s, and three of the SM. S. 81s. These 59 aircraft were followed by an additional 82 machines between August 14 and September 30. Major Alexander von Scheele commanded the German contingent, which grew to a total of 91 officers, airmen, and civilian technicians. In early September, Lieutenant Colonel Walter Warlimont of the German General Staff had replaced von Scheele as Berlin's commander and military advisor to Franco. Within a month's time, the German presence had mushroomed to 600 officers and specialists.

The first Ju 52 transport touched down at Tetuán on July 29, and that very day airlifted a group of Moroccan soldiers to Spain. Once in progress, eleven of these aircraft ferried the bulk of the Army of Africa to Seville or Jeréz de la Frontera during August 1936 and at the completion of this operation in October, the Ju 52s had relocated 13,962 troops and 500 tons of material from Morocco to the mainland.

STALIN'S CHECKMATE

The initial German and Italian intervention in Spain persuaded Joseph Stalin to back the Republic with military assistance. The premier wanted to shield the Popular Front government of France from isolation and encirclement by the fascist powers of Germany and Italy; too, he envisioned a socialist puppet state in Western Europe. Stalin realized, however, that a precipitant diplomatic leap could produce a nasty reversal for the Soviet Union. Involvement in Spain could also hinder his plans to purge the Bolshevik Old Guard regulars. On August 23 Stalin agreed to the conditions of the Non-Intervention Agreement, but behind everything the compelling need of the Spanish Loyalists for arms and the stridency of isolationist groups in even sympathetic Popular Front countries made Russian involvement a foregone conclusion.

On September 10, 1936, 33 Soviet Air Force advisors arrived at Cartagena and began their duties at the surrounding airfields of Carmoli and Los Alcazares. Preparations were made for the arrival of 18 crated I-15 ("I" denotes "Istrebitely," or "Fighter") Russian pursuits, which were being loaded aboard the Soviet freighter *Bolshevik* at Odessa. The vessel reached

Cartagena on October 13, and the Polikarpov biplanes were removed and transported to Los Alcazares for assembly. On the 16th, another Red freighter rendezvoused on the high seas with a Spanish government cargo ship, which hoisted another dozen I-15s aboard and proceeded to Cartagena. That very day, 150 additional Soviet Air personnel under the command of Colonel Yakob Schmouskievich—who carried the nom de guerre "General Douglas" throughout Moscow's adventure in Spain—touched down at an aerodrome south of Alicante. This delegation included 50 combat flyers, and due to their presence the I-15 Chatos debuted over Madrid.

The Red Air Group took Insurgent pilots by surprise, and identification of the new Polikarpov fighters and swift Tupolev SB-2 bombers caused great confusion. Aerial combat involving I-15s first took place on November 4 when ten of these Soviet fighters attacked an Italian reconnaissance plane over the Manzanares River. The spotter plane escaped, but its Fiat fighter escorts were shot down. Other Italian pilots who arrived on the scene as the Chatos were leaving for home mistakenly identified the Polikarpov biplanes as American Curtiss F9C Sparrowhawks. As the civil war progressed, Nationalist combat pilots would also mislabel the Polikarpov I-16 monoplane fighter as a U.S. Boeing P-26A and the Soviet-built SB-2 Tupolev light bomber as the "Martin," due to its resemblance to the American Martin 139 twin-engine bomber. These repeated errors, often widely circulated even by Loyalist volunteers (the worst offenders being the Americans), caused no end of trouble for the U.S. State Department.

Whatever these fighters and other Russian machines may have been called, by the end of 1936, 25 I-15s and 31 I-16s were combat ready and poised around Madrid's perimeter. During October and November, in addition to the Red pursuits circling the capital, 30 I-15s were dispatched to the Basque zone, as well as 31 SB-2 bombers and 31 R-5 "Rasante" reconnaissance and ground-attack biplanes sent to the Madrid front. Concomitantly, the initial groups of multinational ground force volunteers were arriving in Republican Spain to enlist in the International Brigades. Subsequently numbering 33,000, the early battalions went into action at the beginning of November, in conjunction with the appearance of Soviet fighters over Madrid. General Douglas' fighter umbrella put an end to Franco's daylight bombing of the city, and by December 15 the Generalissimo's Madrid offensive had sputtered and ground to a halt.

MAGIC FIRE

The main German intervention in Spain, code-named Unternehmen Zauberfeuer (Operation Magic Fire), had been set in motion by a specially created Sonderstab W (Special Staff W). The Italians, who had not organized their contingent (which was called Operazioni Militari Spagna, or OMS) as carefully, had drafted men and aircraft into the Spanish Foreign Legion. Soviet meddling, however, compelled Hitler to dispatch a full-scale volunteer unit to Spain. In mid-November the Germans crafted the Condor Legion under General Hugo Sperrle, an all-German army with three staffeln of Ju 52 transports, three of outdated Heinkel He 51s, one reconnaissance staffeln with He 70s and He 45s and a seestaffel with He 59 floatplanes plus anti-aircraft guns and ground support personnel. The Condor Legion itself was technically under the operational control of General Alfredo Kindelán, chief of the burgeoning Nationalist Air Force. Actually, the imperious General Sperrle answered only to Franco and thus held rank equivalent to an air theater commander. Sperrle established his headquarters at Seville, commandeered the best hotel there for his personal use, and displayed the swastika flag over it. The general followed this same course of action when he moved his base of operations to Burgos. There he reserved the best brothels for his men, who marched to them—to the amusement of the Spanish prostitutes.

Berlin dictated that the Legion was to be kept at 100 first-line aircraft, complimented with artillery, tanks, communications, and extensive training units. Its mature size would approximate 5,000 troops and airmen. The Italian Aviazione del Tercio was reformed into a full Aviazione Legionaria over the winter of 1936–37, to include three Fiat CR 32 fighter squadriglie, two of S. 81 bombers, and one equipped with Ro 37 reconnaissance craft. Sufficient numbers of Fiat pursuits were made available to form a complete Spanish escuadrilla. Rome's overall contribution of aircraft amounted to 250 machines as well as the CTV (Corpo Truppi Voluntarii), a ground expeditionary force several divisions strong.

FRANCO'S AIRMEN

Spanish combat airmen on both sides of the conflict were dogfighting and bombarding one another months before the formation of the Condor Legion and the Aviazione Legionaria. As early as August 15, Captains Luis Rambaud and Joaquín García Morato, together with Lieutenants García

Pardo, Julio Salvador, and Ramiro Pascual, took possession of the first Heinkel He 51 fighters to arrive in Spain. The Luftwaffe aviators/instructors who had accompanied the He 51s to Spain (ObLt. Kraft Eberhard, HpTm. Hannes Trautloft, HpTm. Herwig Knüppel, HpTm. Ottheinrich von Houwald, Lt. Alfons Klein, and Lt. Ekkehard Hefter), also requested permission to fly combat against Republican fighters. With German approval, General Alfredo Kindelán, chief of the Nationalist Air Services at this time, agreed. Subsequent Spanish pilot error, which caused damage to the undercarriage of the Heinkels during landing, prompted the Germans to petition Kindelán to permit them alone to fly the biplane fighters, a request that was once again allowed. Lieutenant Kraft Eberhard's patrol destroyed six Loyalist machines in mid-August.

When the Spanish squadron was disbanded at the end of August 1936, Captains Rambaud and Morato applied for transfer to the regular Nationalist Air Force, Salvador and Pascual to the Italian Legion. General Kindelán refused all applications. Morato and Salvador flew the He 51s again on September 2 during the Battle of Talavera de la Reina.

Although the breakup of the Rambaud squadron caused disappointment to its members, the fact that the Spaniards and Germans had been living and fighting together in relative harmony was encouraging for the future of the Nationalist war effort. In addition, Morato's promising record in any and all fighter aircraft showed that any gifted Spanish combat pilot could compete against anyone in the skies over Spain. Still, there were prejudiced German aviators and technicians who believed that their very presence in Iberia documented the Spanish military's inability to master new technology. Moreover, the Luftwaffe representatives abhorred what they saw as the Latin fighter pilot's penchant for frontal aerial encounters, as opposed to the employment of maneuver, deception, and flank assault.

MORATO

Joaquín García Morato y Castano had been an accomplished pilot long before the Nationalist insurrection. He entered the Toledo military school at an early age; and on graduation as second lieutenant, he was assigned to an infantry regiment in Spanish Morocco. At twenty years of age, Morato transferred to the Spanish Air Force and participated in combat toward the end of the Moroccan War; his de Havilland DH 9 was twice shot down by ground fire without injury to its pilot. Following the armistice, Morato wangled a transfer to the seaplane base at Melilla. Shortly thereafter, he crashed into the Mediterranean while stunting, breaking several bones and nearly drowning in the process. The young flyer recuperated at the Carabanchel hospital near Madrid. After a year's hiatus, he joined a reconnaissance squadron based at Getafe. Scarcely there any time, Morato moved on to the aviation school at Alcalá de Henares, where he took part in the first Blind Flying Course. Morato next learned aerobatics on his own and subsequently competed internationally in a number of contests, winning top honors wherever he went, and becoming renowned for stunt flying in Spain. By 1930 Morato had climbed to a fighter instructorship at Alcalá.

With the civil war in full flower, Morato found himself in London on holiday. Back in France, he tried to cross into Spain at Irún, but the frontier, still in Loyalist hands, was closed to him. He finagled a small plane, however, and flew to Burgos, arriving there on August 2, 1936. Morato learned that his parents were trapped in Madrid, but that his wife and four children had escaped from Málaga to Gibraltar. Morato had a huge score to settle with the Reds.

He undertook his first combat sortie on August 3 in an obsolete Nieuport-Delage 52. On August 12 he notched his first "kill," a Vickers Vildebeeste, and on ensuing days he prevented the swift Russian SB-2 bombers from unloading over Córdoba. During his stint with the Rambaud squadron, Morato claimed three more victories.

On his days off from fighter duty, Morato assisted his brother-in-law, Carlos Haya, as co-pilot in a Ju 52 bomber. Together they bombed the aerodrome at Cuatro Vientos on the nights of August 27 and 28, as well as the station at Villalba on the latter date, where the pair destroyed an ammunition dump. That same evening, Morato and Captain Baron Rudolph von Moreau dropped a 250-kilogram bomb on the patio of the Loyalist War Ministry even as the minister and his cabinet were in session. An inner wall collapsed on this august assemblage, but without loss of life. The surprise raid, nevertheless, garnered significant propaganda value.

IL DUCE'S EAGLES

On September 5, Captain Vincenzo Dequal arrived in Seville to assume command of the first Fiat squadron. Morato immediately approached the captain's superior for permission to hunt with the Dequal group. From the outset, Morato liked Dequal, or "Limonesi" as his men called him, and under his leadership morale remained high and coordination excellent.

The Spanish ace joined Dequal's unit on September 6, and three days later there were sufficient Fiats to have a squadron transferred to Cáceres. The three Tablada patrols within the group were led by Dequal, Morato, and Adriano Montelli (who left Spain with a dozen confirmed and three unconfirmed victories). On September 11, Dequal's squadron went into combat with great success, destroying two Breguet 19s and five Loyalist fighters. For his part, Morato downed a Nieuport 52 over Talavera, recording his first "kill" in a Fiat. Several days later (September 13), he shared two victories with Italian comrades. Again, on September 16, Morato and Montelli's patrols flamed a Breguet, two fighters, and a Potez 54 near Navalcarnero.

During the September 13 dogfight, García Morato lost a comrade in the person of Vincent Patriarca, alias Vincenza Bocalare, an Italian-American volunteer who had been in Spain scarcely two weeks. In this engagement Franco's only known American pilot shared two kills with the Spanish ace and Montelli before having to bail out himself over Republican territory.

When information reached the U.S. State Department that Patriarca was in custody and condemned to death, the American Embassy in Spain was directed to interview him. Back home the affair caused a brief media uproar. Both President Franklin Roosevelt and the State Department were flooded with communications asking that Patriarca's life be spared. In mid-October a hopeful initiative promised the Italian-American's release from a Loyalist jail in exchange for a Yugoslav pilot, but the negotiations went nowhere.

Ultimately, the Spanish minister of state announced that the Republic could not guarantee Patriarca's safety, and together with mounting pressure from the United States, his release was ordered on November 6. Three weeks later Patriarca embarked for home.

SALAS AND SALVADOR JOIN THE ITALIANS

At this juncture, the brilliant flyers Angel Salas Larrazábal and Julio Salvador Diaz Benjumea materialized at Tablada offering to serve with Dequal's Italians. Salas, an artillery lieutenant in 1926, graduated to the air service and became a pilot in 1929. At the end of 1930, Salas went to Africa, stationed initially at Tetuán. Promoted to captain in February 1936, he served at Cabo Juby until the civil war when he returned to Spain. His first assignment was to liaise between Generals Mola, Franco, and Queipo de Llano; after this service he migrated to the Nationalist Nieuport 52 Squadron, winning his first combat victory at Teruel. Julio Salvador Diaz Benjumea also began his career in the artillery in 1930 and later became a student pilot at Albacete. His airmanship won him a post with the Seville Nieuport 52 Squadron and later assignment to a fighter unit at Granada. Salvador flew Nieuports until the Heinkel fighters arrived in Seville, at which time he joined the Rambaud squadron. On August 18, Salvador claimed his first and second victories. Initially there were questions about the credentials of these two Spaniards, but after Salas' aerobatics demonstration, including stunts which even the Italians had not tried in their Fiats, the Dequal squadron accepted their Latin allies with open arms.

On November 5 came the first huge aerial battle of the war. Nine Fiats from Torrijones (pilots including Morato, Salas, and Salvador) encountered fifteen Chatos and several Potezs between Leganés and Madrid. Spurning the possibility of reinforcements from Talavera, the group commander attacked. Morato destroyed an I-15 and disabled a Potez bomber, forcing it to land. Salas flamed a Chato and placed two additional Polikarpovs *hors combat* southeast of Barajas. Coming under fire himself, Salas dived and made his getaway at treetop level. Four days later, three squadrons of Romeos, Ju 52s, and Fiat strafers made as many sorties to the Manzanares River. During the final mission, 14 Fiats tangled with two squadrons of I-15s from Barajas and Alcalá with two Red fighters shot down. Morato accounted for one of the Chatos, making this his fourteenth victory.

On November 13, above the Pasco de Rosales (Madrid), 14 Fiats dueled with government Chatos. Morato destroyed an I-15, Salas crippled three and forced them to land, and Salvador flamed another. On their return flight, the threesome came across five SB-2 "Katiuskas" plastering Getafe and Cuatro Vientos airfields from a height of 16,500 feet. Salas sent one SB-2 crew bailing out of their riddled bomber, and Morato damaged three other "Katiuskas." On that day, the Spanish ace recorded his fifteenth "kill," both Salas and Salvador their fifth. In this engagement, a downed Soviet Chato pilot who parachute-landed in Madrid was beaten to death by a mob whose leaders mistook him for a German. Commander Dequal and his wingman were shot down in a separate aerial melee. Wounded, the Italian dropped by parachute between the lines.

From December 2 to 15, 1936, the Fiat group had suffered disproportionate losses among its Italian aviators. Of the original squadron commanders, all had been lost through injury, death, or imprisonment by the enemy. Morato counted six dead among the Italian airmen, and three languished in Red prisons. Worst of all, the wounded Dequal had been rotated back to Italy. By some miracle and good flying, the three Spanish officers of these squadrons—Captains Morato, Salas, and Lieutenant Salvador—all remained uninjured during their tour with the Italian group.

THE BLUE PATROL

Morato and Salas grew restive under Legion orders that Rebel fighters were forbidden to cross Republican lines. Day-by-day the situation deteriorated as Dequal's successor, Captain Tarscisco Fagnani, stood his ground. Finally, Salas, who was leading a patrol, ignored the directive. Fagnani tried to have the Spaniard arrested when he returned to base, but Morato argued that in Spain nobody was arrested for showing courage. The result of subsequent meetings between Morato and Salas was a decision to establish their own independent squadron. On December 22, Morato took French leave and flew to Seville. Operating from Córdoba the next day, he gave support to the Insurgent advance on Porcuna and Lopera. Salvador followed Morato on Christmas Eve, and a comrade, Narcisco Bermudez de Castro, joined them immediately. The Blue Patrol, or "La Patrulla Azul," had become a reality. Captain Salas and Lieutenant García Pardo remained in the Italian Fiat group through the New Year, but in early January they also moved to the south.

THE ABRAHAM LINCOLN BATTALION

The deployment of the International Brigades in Spain constituted great propaganda for the Republic in particular and the worldwide Popular Front effort in general. In the fall of 1936, the Comintern sanctioned the enlistment of foreigners for military duty in Spain. Across the United States, the Communists recruited in such representative unions as the seamen and longshoremen, miners, steelworkers, and automobile assemblymen. Targeted professions in the world of letters included teachers, graduate students, writers, artists, and other members of the intelligentsia whose members were willing to embark on a grand crusade against fascism. Jewish enlistees accounted for 30 percent of the U.S. Internationals, and Afro-Americans numbered around one hundred volunteers. The Internationals hailed from the large cities of the Northeast, the Pacific Coast, the Midwest, and Northwest, where organized labor held sway and left-wing politics flourished. In Europe, deep-seated class antagonisms fostered by economic depression and bleak market conditions drove workers into the arms of the Communist recruiters. Motivated, too, by this global financial depression, most Americans, nevertheless, went to Spain as part of a grand crusade against fascism.

Once in Spain, the Americans formed a component of the XVth

International Brigade (IB), also including English and Canadian troops. With the arrival of sixty U.S. citizens in Barcelona early in January 1937, the State Department immediately sought to cut off this flow of volunteers. A clause in the U.S. Code forbade open recruiting inside the country. Moreover, legislation enacted thirty years earlier prohibited Americans from pledging allegiance to a foreign power under the threat of loss of citizenship. From those individuals who went abroad, the State Department required an affidavit declaring that they did not intend to travel to Spain.

Circumvention proved to be all too easy. Americans went to Europe and were recruited on foreign soil. Also, the Republicans did not always require a formal oath of allegiance, as there were other holds on these volunteers and mercenaries. For instance, passports were collected by recruiters in France. This requirement made it difficult for the American, alone, to return to the United States (or to travel to any other European nation) without the suggestion of Spanish Civil War involvement. Finally, President Franklin Roosevelt tended to cast a benign eye on violations of the U.S. neutrality position during the conflict's early stage.

In the winter of 1936–37, the Abraham Lincoln sobriquet referred to a single battalion within the XVth International Brigade. Such battalions of 400–700 men were the basic components of the five brigades and organized along national and/or linguistic lines. Approximately 35,000 foreigners from 53 countries fought in the International Brigades. Over time, these men (and women) found their sacrifices to be "expected," their drill hard, their officers careless with human life, and their daily diet of chickpeas and burro meat unappetizing. The volatile commandant of the IBs, French Communist André Marty, referred to Americans as "spoiled crybabies" because of their incessant complaints. The Lincoln and other IB units were used as elite "shock troops," expended to inspire Spanish regulars and militia with their skill and dash. These battalions were employed to plug gaps in Loyalist lines at a horrifying loss of life. During the Jarama campaign in early 1937, the IBs were ordered to perform near-suicidal charges.

3

POLIKARPOVS OVER SPAIN

> In a fighter plane . . . we have found a way to return to war as it ought to be, war which is individual combat between two people in which one either kills or is killed. It's exciting, it's individual, and it's disinterested.
>
> Richard Hillary
> RAF Pilot

Uncle Sam's prodigal flyers-for-hire were a different breed from the earthbound brigaders. Spain offered them a greater chance for international recognition, perhaps even a footnote in history. There they might test their God-given and acquired skills, tap inner emotional reserves, enrich themselves, passionately defend a country against the proxies of totalitarianism, carouse with flamboyant fellow adventurers, spin yarns, pilot formidable aircraft, and shoot down others of similar mettle.

The decade between the end of the Great War and the beginning of the Great Depression afforded aviators few opportunities for earning a living in the air: mail runs, barnstorming, air shows, and flying lessons sold to gaping yokels in America's heartland put food on the table, but for dedicated pilots it was the initial prospect of pay for flying and the hunt that sent them abroad. For a large number of the U.S. flyers, and especially Tinker, personal involvement grew to be a question of idealism, mirroring an inner revulsion against the antidemocratic, anti-Semitic, anti-union, anti-intellectual, and all-around misanthropic tenets of fascism. From this perspective, these flyers were no more ideological than their countrymen;

rather, all seemed to share the unsettling belief that something sinister was afoot in the world and that time was running out for the democracies.

There seemed to be an even deeper compulsion, however, that spurred these men on to Spain. Over the course of their respective lives, some of them had allowed marriages to founder, budding careers to languish, and fortunes to go aglimmering, but not one of them surrendered his zest for flying and adventure. Flight and the chance for combat meant jailbreak, freedom from all those mundane, soul-destroying responsibilities that chained them down at home; it also symbolized the possible antidote to a lifetime of anonymity and failure—the enduring promise of personal and professional renewal. Flight exalted solitude, cunning, and indifference, the virtues of wolves.

HIGH TIDE

The first American volunteer flyers set foot in Spain on September 24, 1936. This contingent included Eugene Finick, Joseph Rosmarin, Ed Lyons, Arthur Shapiro, and Benjamin David Leider. Both Shapiro and Finick were students of Lyons, a flight instructor from Floyd Bennett Field in New York. A second wave of U.S. pilots reached Spain on or before November 20. They were: Bert Acosta, Gordon Berry, Edward Schneider, Edwin Semons, Frederick Ives Lord, Vincent Schmidt, and Hilaire du Berrier, an American expatriate residing in England. The largest and most qualified body of aviators came in December and went straight to the Republican Air Ministry in Valencia. These men were in order of their arrivals: Charles Koch and James Allison on the ninth; Derek Dickinson, Manuel Gomez, and Orrin Bell on the twenty-first; Albert Baumler on the twenty-fourth; Nord Caldwell and Sam Brenner on the twenty-fifth; Harold Dahl on the twenty-eighth; and Frank Tinker on January 3, 1937.

The methods of recruitment employed to snare these mercenaries were varied and informal. Those airmen who came to Spain in September were enlisted by the Communist Party in New York City. Madrid's recruiting agent, Ed Semons, sent the candidates to New York City attorney Sam Schacter, who, as go-between for the Spanish consulate, gave them passage and expense money to sail to France. Among the December group, Dickinson, Bell, Brenner, Caldwell, and Koch were solicited in New York City by the Socialist Workers' Party. Dickinson, Bell, and Manuel Gomez were chaperoned to Spain by the Spanish national Augustin Sanz Sainz. Sainz made travel arrangements for the three flyers and planned for their transit to Valencia via France. For his good offices, Sainz would become the subsecretary of Air for the Republican government. The great majority of these expatriates regarded the Communist and Socialist parties as guarantors of their safe passage to Spain and nothing more.

Madrid's requirements were straightforward: (1) at least 2,500 hours in the air, preferably military flying; (2) nothing pro-fascist in a volunteer's background; and (3) the candidate must show a record of loyalty to whomever he served in the past. An exception was made in the case of Fred Lord. Although he once participated in a "good revolution" in Mexico, Lord also flew for the White Russians in the anti-Soviet campaigns following the Bolshevik revolution. This violation of Madrid's rule was ignored, however, due to the mercenary's reputation for reliability and ability.

Of the September arrivals, all were flight tested and found to be unsuitable for combat; despite their shortcomings, these men were paid to fly transports. Ben Leider, Gene Finick, and Ed Lyons eventually saw combat, a victory some of their comrades attributed to their endurance and perseverance as much as additional flying experience.

THE SEPTEMBER FLYERS

As a Jew and a Communist, Ben Leider came to Spain to fight for the underdog against tyranny and injustice; he invariably perceived the world in black and white, as gray was never his color. The thirty-five-year-old aviator grew up in Kishinev, formerly a part of Russia and later absorbed into Romania. During his boyhood, Ben witnessed the Kishinev massacre. This pogrom stemmed from the revolutionary uprisings of 1905 and Czar Nicholas' ruthless suppression of them.

His family migrated to New York City where the elder Leider obtained work as a common laborer. Ben posted high marks at PS 109 in Brooklyn, and, although known for his precociousness, he was equally good with his fists. At fourteen he worked on the West Street docks. While at Commercial High School, young Leider won medals for track, cross-country, rowing, and wrestling; his passion, however, was writing for the school newspaper.

In order to enter the College of the City of New York in 1920, Leider crammed two years of required courses into one. In his junior year, he switched to the journalism school of the University of Missouri. He spent his spare time as the "hiking reporter" for the Columbia *Missourian*. Leider's distaste for racial bigotry came across in an account of a lynching; likewise, the aspiring reporter's admiration for Eugene V. Debs, the Socialist leader, was equally evident in his coverage of the reformer's rallies. In 1927 Leider embarked for the Soviet Union, and, with notebook and camera, he documented the average Russian's improved condition under Red leadership. Charles A. Lindbergh's transatlantic flight that same year fired his imagination. With borrowed funds and a partner, he purchased a J-4 Cessna. In no time, Leider developed into a competent pilot, and, with his pilot's license in hand, he mastered aerial photography.

Between 1930 and 1934, Leider worked for the New York City News Association, a reporting service for municipal papers, and for the government's Works Progress Administration. In these jobs, he covered everything from the plight of coal miners in Harlan, Kentucky to slum conditions right at home. In nearly every story, he managed to weave in a detailed proletarian bias.

The New York *Post* welcomed Leider in 1934 as its "flying reporter." No matter the weather, he always flew to where the news broke: the Morro Castle story, the Bruno Hauptmann trial, the celebrities aboard the Hindenburg and the Queen Mary. From the air, Leider dived down near his subject, and, with his knees controlling the joystick, he snapped air photos with his camera. Of course, he accepted a charter membership in the Newspaper Guild. In the throes of his union's first strike against the Long Island *Press*, Leider affixed a huge "Join the Guild" caption on his plane and circled low over the publisher's roof. He spent his vacation in 1936 flying cross-country to protest William Randolph Hearst's *Wisconsin News* and helped accomplish a Guild victory, the fruits of which extended to all of the Hearst syndicate papers. With more than a hint of bitterness in his voice, he would personalize to a fellow striker his dedication to America's working class: "My mother damned near killed herself working so her kids would have schoolbooks and get an education, and I'm not one of those guys who forget where they came from when they get some middle-class job and start eating regular."

When the Spanish unpleasantness erupted, Leider answered the call. September volunteer Art Shapiro, alias Arturo Vasnit, reported that trainee Leider's flight checks were less than spectacular. Poor Leider's landings in behemoth Breguet 19s were too slow, too long in duration, and frequently resulted in collapsed undercarriages. André Malraux's chief pilot, who oversaw the practice, winced at the sight of him. Attempting to uphold the honor of his countrymen, in the face of Leider's sorry performances, Shapiro once circled the aerodrome for 63 landing approaches within an hour's time.

Despite these inauspicious beginnings, Leider was assigned to pilot a Lockheed-Vega transport, and for months he crisscrossed Iberia's skies carrying military brass and munitions, flying from Valencia to Albacete, Alicante, and Madrid. Leider's total commitment to the Republic and his optimism for a successful conclusion of the conflict can be appreciated in his letter to his brother Will, dated December 28, 1936. Living in a Spanish nobleman's palace and writing on the former owner's stationery, bearing the fascist's coat-of-arms, he concluded: "The sanctimonious parasite beat it when things got hot. . . . Don't worry. I have more than enough of everything, and I wouldn't miss the show here for all the weeping of all the mothers in the world."

Leider's pleas for a pursuit plane were rejected over and over until he threatened to steal one. In February 1937 his commandant capitulated and sent him to combat school for two weeks of special training. He stayed one week and reported for duty at Alcalá de Henares just north of Madrid. It has been suggested that the Soviet Air Force authorities in Spain, perhaps even "General Douglas," pressured the Air Ministry to assign Leider a combat role. Over García LaCalle's objection, Leider was sent to his squadron. No doubt the Russians saw him as perfect for one of two roles: hero or martyr.

Joe Rosmarin of Brooklyn, New York, also pulled transport duty, and in one fifteen-day stint he logged well over one hundred hours. His wife, Pauline, could speak Russian, English, Spanish, French, and Yiddish. She served as interpreter for Yacob Schmouskievich (General Douglas). Known by his alias, Jaime Field, Rosmarin remained in Spain until November 1937.

Ed Lyons and Art Shapiro began as transport jockeys, but soon graduated to bomber duty. Known as Ed Lebowitz in Spain, Lyons contracted to fly bombers on November 11, and was assigned to pilot Soviet Rasantes (Grupo 15) at Quintanar. In this role, he performed bombing and strafing raids in both the R-5 groundstrafers and the Czech Aero 100s. Shapiro considered his bomber patrols as humdrum, and the money afforded little inducement to stay. The Republican Air Ministry finally promoted him to the swift SB-2 Russian "Katiuska" bombers. Taking his orders from a Soviet base commander with the assistance of an interpreter, he guided himself to the target with the help of faded photocopies of tourist road maps. With his Spanish crew, Shapiro communicated only by two lights: red for left, green for right. The majority of his sixteen missions were to bomb Toledo. Rebel flak patterns lay at either 5,000 or 15,000 feet, so he dealt death unruffled from 10,000 feet above his victims. Since Shapiro did not realize that the historic Alcázar fortress was in Toledo, his routine objective meant little to him. Worst of all, Shapiro could never tell what, if anything, he hit on the ground.

At twenty-five, Eugene Finick found himself immersed in a foreign civil war. Of Czech-Polish ancestry, this New York City Catholic had experienced a difficult youth. With his father's death, Finick left school to support his mother and three siblings. Five days a week, he labored as an auto mechanic, but on weekends he took flying lessons at Floyd Bennett and Roosevelt airports—the cost defrayed by a mentor and friends. Finick lacked the money for a professional pilot's license, so he would leave for Spain with only a student's certificate. What this novice pilot lacked on paper, however, he made up for in anti-fascist zeal. When disputes arose among his circle of flyers as to which side was morally right in Spain, he backed the Republic. During one such argument, Finick signed a recruiter's contract on the tarmac of Floyd Bennett Field and proceeded overseas.

Following his preliminary flight checks, Finick's outfit gave air support to Loyalist militias attempting to forestall Franco's march to relieve Toledo's Alcázar garrison. On November 1, his unit was rotated back to Murcia to await the arrival of Soviet aircraft. Three weeks later the Chatos came, and Finick heaved a sigh of relief with these deadly little biplanes flying escort duty for his bombers. His good fortune continued when, on January 10, he won assignment to a squadron of R-5 "Rasante" groundstrafers. It was in a Rasante that Finick made his debut as pilot on the central front in the middle of January 1937.

THE NOVEMBER FLYERS

After the departure of the September volunteers, the recruiters located additional aviators with plenty of enthusiasm, but with little combat flying experience. Twenty-six-year-old Ed Semons, an avid student of flying, stepped in to lend his support. He regularly motored over to Floyd Bennett Field, where everyone knew him and regarded him as an oddity. Semons approached Bert Acosta and company and offered them all jobs at $1,500 a month. The pilots all laughed, but the next day they signed contracts. With Semons as guide, the delegation sailed on November 11. Once in Europe, Semons established headquarters in Paris and Valencia, flying between cities chaperoning additional recruits.

This group of airmen checked out as bomber pilots and received orders to proceed to the Basque front. These November volunteers aggravated their Spanish superiors as much on the ground as they did in the air. Drunken brawls and missed assignments became commonplace. Acosta enjoyed flying with a brandy bottle in one hand and his smokes in the other. His pals confided to a U.S. Embassy official that Acosta possessed such rare flying ability that it was unnecessary for him to remain conscious while on a combat mission. Their cheeky testimonial barely captured Acosta's brilliant flying career, and, despite his erratic behavior, this handsome, genial, alcoholic womanizer commanded the respect of his peers. Over the course of his life, he had been a barnstormer, speed racer, test pilot, aeronautical engineer, civilian flight instructor to Canadian flyboys during World War I, failed entrepreneur, and always the aerial clown. Legend had it that Acosta once buzzed a huge clock on a New York City skyscraper when a passenger asked for the time. Who could forget his role as Richard E. Byrd's pilot-of-choice on the commander's famous transatlantic flight of 1927?

On November 28, Acosta, Lord, Berry, and Schneider, together with two Englishmen, were dispatched to Sondica Airfield near Bilbao. The aerodrome lay just three miles from Lamiaco, where their Russian fighter cover was based. Acosta took his rest and relaxation at Biarritz, a French resort across the frontier. Assigned to a Potez 54 bomber squadron under the command of Manuel Cascon Briega, the Americans were flabbergasted at the conditions there and the dangerous civil planes that they were expected to man. Fred Lord observed: "That hanger contained two English Miles sport jobs, a couple of Monospars with tiny Pobjoy motors, an old cabin Farman with a J-6 motor, a Vickers two-seater reconnaissance job with a prop that looked like a telephone pole, a J-6 Fokker tri-motor passenger plane, and two Breguet two-place bombers of 1925 vintage." In other hangers, the Americans found old Nieuports, Loires, Potezs, and World War I de Havillands. Finick groused: "We'd have taken planes out of the Smithsonian."

From the start, things went badly as Fred Lord tried to demonstrate the fragility of his machine to the Republican officers. Who better to plead the group's case than this World War I ace? A lifelong roustabout and adventurer, Lord ran away from school in 1916 to join Texas infantry on the Mexican border. Within the next year, he enlisted with the Royal Canadian Flying Corps and flew in France until he was shot down two days before the Armistice. In the harrowing interim, Lord bagged nine enemy aircraft. As a mercenary, he fought with the Whites in postwar Russia and subsequently worked his way through two revolutions in Mexico and one in Central America.

Back at Sondica Airfield, Lord took his commander aloft in a Breguet 19 and reached 2,000 feet when the upper wing collapsed. The officer nervously motioned for him to climb higher so that they could use their parachutes, but Lord refused, knowing that ground crewmen liked to sleep on silk chutes spread out on the damp floor of hangers, and that wet silk does not open easily. Instead, he tried a landing with the biplane's damaged wing. No sooner had they touched down, than the Spaniard ordered Lord arrested; Lord barely escaped being shot.

The Air Ministry's November "enlistees" were to bomb Rebel batteries some 75 miles away over country that would not forgive an emergency landing. The Americans drew no flying togs. Acosta flew in the same rumpled suit he had worn to Spain. His own light topcoat served to protect him against the wind and rain. The foursome manned lumbering Potez 54s, obsolete bombers devoid of any real defensive protection. Neighboring Soviet airmen took pity on their allies and offered them flight suits, sidearms, and escort protection whenever possible. The San Sebastian Pursuit Squadron, a forerunner of the Condor Legion with its Heinkel 51 fighters, made life hell for Acosta's Potez outfit.

Worst still, on occasion the "Suicide Patrol" flew raids in rickety Breguet cabin barges retired from France's civilian airlines. The pilot carried a pistol for protection, and the observer packed a rifle against enemy pursuits. The latter secured himself to the floor of the Breguet and poked his head through a hole cut in the top fabric of the fuselage; assuming this comic position, the observer/gunner could fire at hostile fighters. At a maximum speed of 120 miles per hour, there was no chance of the Breguets outrunning their Heinkel pursuers.

On a particular sortie against an enemy airfield at Vitoria, a covey of German Heinkels assailed Acosta's converted bombers with a singleminded viciousness. Before the bomber crew members could react, Britisher Sydney Holland, who flew at the end of the formation, lost his machine and crashed. In his attempt to follow the Englishman down, Acosta became encircled by enemy fighters. Out of this engagement emerged one of the more remarkable war stories of the Spanish Civil War.

From behind, Acosta could hear his Spanish gunner blazing away at the Germans while singing off-color ditties. A Luftwaffe pilot drew alongside to inspect Acosta's bomber before dropping away to shoot it down. In the twinkling of an eye "Aviation's Bad Boy" whipped out his revolver and shot the German in the face. Meanwhile his gunner nailed another Heinkel pilot on his portside, and both enemy planes plunged to earth side by side. As a third Heinkel lined up behind the Breguet for the kill, Acosta's rifleman shot him in the throat and his biplane trailed after the black spirals of his squadronmates. The last He 51 fled. Back at the base, Acosta and his observer demanded their bonus money; instead of cash and congratulations, they received a chilly rebuff. Could they prove their destruction of three Heinkels? No confirmation—no bonus money! Acosta realized that he was waging a losing battle.

It was in the Basque province of northwestern Spain that Acosta, Berry, Schneider, and Lord decided to end their association with the Republic. The mercenaries hired a boat to smuggle them across the Bay of Biscay to Biarritz, France. The scheme fell apart at the last minute: the boatman shot and the would-be deserters dragged before Air Ministry brass in Valencia. The ensuing interrogation abruptly ended with Acosta being physically ejected from the building. Their irate Spanish employers provided the four with severance papers and partial pay in pesetas (non-exportable currency) before escorting them to the French border. From France, the outcasts embarked for America. Back home, the Acosta crew told their side of the Spanish fiasco to the press. Federal agents seized their passports and hauled the flyers before a grand jury investigating U.S. aviators in Spain. State Department officials resurrected the 1907 law dissolving the citizenship of any American who had "taken an oath of allegiance to any foreign state." The Acosta group had dodged this proverbial bullet by swearing allegiance to the Loyalist Air Ministry, so the four detainees were freed.

In early January, Acosta and Berry temporarily convinced the U.S. Coast Guard to serve a writ on a Spanish Republican ship, the *Mar Cantábrico*, which was then anchored in Long Island Sound. Nothing occurred, the vessel weighed anchor and sailed, and it was eventually attacked and captured by the Nationalists, who took it as a prize and killed its crew. The mercenaries' main attempt to seize Loyalist property in lieu of bonus money made front page news in most American papers, and this international incident gave Washington more ammunition in support of its non-intervention policies.

As previously noted, the December arrivals were flight tested and sent to Manises Airfield on the outskirts of Valencia for Breguet 19 bomber training. At Manises, the Yanks found themselves in an Anglo-U.S. squadron. Unfortunately, incessant bickering and competitive rancor between British airmen and their colonial counterparts forced the Air Ministry to disperse the Americans among other units. Sam Brenner alone stayed with the Breguet team as a gunner/mechanic. Combat-tested Al Baumler went to a Russian Chato squadron, and Tinker, Dahl, Leider, Gomez, Koch, and Allison were sent to the Escuadrilla de Chatos commanded by twenty-two-year-old Andres García LaCalle. The ace of the Government air service with eleven victories and the hero of the Talavera battles, reports had it that LaCalle destroyed five Nationalist machines in one day. His understudies were sent to Los Alcazares for training in the Polikarpov I-15.

4

LA PATRULLA AMERICANA

> We'll go up to the sun; it will be warm there. And remember, try to keep them off my tail and I'll try to do the same for you.
>
> O. D. Bell to Manuel Gomez
> February 1937

> During the long summer days when the light was crystal clear they flew long before the sun painted the sombre hills; and they flew again and again, half-naked, their bodies oil-stained, their faces blackened from the gun ports, until the light began to fade.
>
> James Edgar Johnson
> *The Story of Air Fighting*

On January 19, 1937, Tinker and company were told that they would become part of an all-Spanish combat squadron. The Republic wanted all-Spanish squadrons in an attempt to free itself of Soviet dominance in the air; heretofore, if Russian commanders opposed a particular military operation, they summarily withheld support. The Government believed that a preponderance of Spanish aircrews would result in greater control of its own air force. As an early precedent, the Air Ministry created the first "all-Spanish" Chato squadron. Because there were not enough native pilots to man the Polikarpovs, volunteers Koch, Allison, Dahl, Leider, and Tinker joined twelve Spanish aviators to form the LaCalle squadron at Los Alcazares on January 23.

LaCalle and the prehistoric Nieuport fighter he flew to acedom during the early days of the struggle impressed Tinker to no end:

LaCalle was a tall, slim Spaniard with an unruly mane of very black hair. We found out later that he had shot down eleven German and Italian fighting planes while flying in Nieuports. . . . He had been a sergeant in the regular Spanish Air Corps before the war and had worked his way up to the rank of captain by sheer merit. He had lately been flying the Boeing (I-15) fighters with the Russians and had become very popular with them.

What a plane [Nieuport]! It had a stick that looked like a section of railroad crosstie and the plane itself handled about as easily as an old-time heavy truck. . . . I got out of it with a feeling of astonishment, caused primarily by the fact that I was still alive and secondarily, by the fact that I had found a worse ship than the Breguet.

Tinker soon learned that LaCalle stood for little foolishness when it came to flying, but displayed almost boyish exuberance during off hours. As squadron commander, he rated a car and a driver at his disposal, although he usually drove himself. The rangy Spaniard selected the smallest car that he could find, and the aspect of the vehicle and driver together brought guffaws from his pilots. His passion in wet weather seemed to be driving at top speed across the runway and skidding round and round.

Tinker's instructors decreed that the LaCalle group be formed into three four-plane patrols. Given their choice, the Americans chose to stay together and were known as "La Patrulla Americana." To his everlasting consternation, Tinker discovered that some of LaCalle's Spanish flyers had less than fifty hours flying time, whereas stateside military flying schools required over three times as much trainer experience aloft before one's introduction to fighter aircraft. Since Koch was the eldest and most experienced man in the American Patrol (he boasted a total of 2,285 flying hours when he arrived in Spain) his mates chose him to lead the patrol. Leider, who knew Spanish and fraternized with the native pilots of the squadron, still retained great weight with his fellow countrymen as a moral leader. They, in turn, liked and admired him despite his special treatment by the Communists and his general standoffish demeanor.

The group delighted in the I-15 biplanes, a stubby pursuit craft of 3,150 lbs. and powered by a 700 hp engine. It proved to be a much superior machine to the F4B fighter that Tinker piloted at Pensacola, Florida; whereas the F4B was armed with only two .30 caliber machine guns synchronized to fire through the propeller, the I-15 Chato packed four 7.62 mm guns that ringed the engine. What appealed to Tinker was its nine millimeters of armor, a godsend which U.S. fighter pilots did without until

World War II. The Chato's powerplant, however, was "all-American," a Wright Cyclone engine built under license in the Soviet Union.

La Patrulla Americana flew into history with Koch in the lead, Allison and Tinker in wing positions, and Whitey Dahl flying in No. 4 slot. It was not until toward the end of his preliminary instructional phase that Tinker learned why he had been kept out of a Chato's cockpit for so long a period of time: "It seemed that there were some other American pilots who arrived in Spain drunk, were drunk practically all the time they were there, and were still drunk when they were poured aboard the homeward-bound steamer. Another government might have lined all of them up against the nearest wall." On the final day of January, the LaCalle unit moved from Los Alcazares to the airfield at Alcantarilla, near Murcia, where the pilots were to receive their Chatos. On the eve of the move, Koch came down with stomach trouble, an ailment thought to be induced by the rich Spanish cuisine. In time, the stricken flyer would be diagnosed with a deteriorating stomach ulcer. The flight surgeon held Koch back as the squadron's transfer proceeded. Broken-hearted, the sick pilot saw his comrades off to the front, his seat on the train occupied by a young Spanish aviator known as "Chang" Selles. He bore the moniker "Chang" because of the fact that he had been born and reared in Japan. This remarkable fellow could speak Japanese, English, and Spanish with equal fluency. After a week's recuperation, Koch was summoned elsewhere, so he never actually rejoined the LaCalle outfit.

Captain LaCalle awaited his new charges at Murcia, where he gave them a fight talk and toasted their forthcoming successes with champagne into the wee hours. Alcantarilla's aerodrome was where a foggy-headed Tinker first caressed his ship and met his mechanic the following morning: "The fuselage and wings of my ship had been manufactured in Russia. The motor was a new Wright Cyclone, made in Paterson, New Jersey. My mechanic was a huge and nearsighted Asturian by the name of Chamorro—and I still couldn't roll my double Rs." He gratefully drew a parachute of American manufacture and a complete flying outfit consisting of leather trousers, flying jacket, fur-lined boots, helmet, and gloves. Tinker knew the importance of warm flying togs and a proper parachute. Flying in an open cockpit during winter, the temperature at 5,000 meters up could be as much as 30 degrees below ground temperature. Every morning, ground crews filled the engine radiators with boiling water before going through the ordeal of trying to start the motor. Following a mission, some fighter pilots would have to be helped from their cockpits by ground crewmen. The flyer's legs and hands frequently had no feeling, and it was excruciating for them afterwards thawing out by a fire. The lucky pilots drew the American Irvin seat-pack chutes; the unfortunates made do with a French parachute which stressed the abdomen rather than the shoulders and thighs. It was carried on the chest, with the harness encircling the flyer's sides, thereby producing tremendous abdominal pressure during bailout. The Arkansan had been in war-torn Spain only one month.

SETTLING IN

On February 3, Tinker, Allison, and Dahl purchased several bottles of wine from a neighboring farmer and proceeded to drink and gamble on Alcantarilla's tarmac. After several hours of this recreation, an alarm flare sent the threesome aloft where Tinker, in a state of intoxication, accidently cut his engine and was forced to land back at the airfield. His mechanic uncovered the defect immediately, and, in the face of widespread heckling, the embarrassed Tinker took flight again. Once back in formation, he and Dahl decided to perform some daring aerobatics, literally flying over and under their leader's machine while in formation. At times, Allison had to push their wing tips away from his open cockpit. At Albacete, Tinker violated an unwritten law in Spanish aviation circles by landing before the squadron commander. Once down, La Patrulla Americana was officially welcomed by half the townspeople of Albacete, including a fair sprinkling of politicians and military brass. The American patrol stood before its grateful hosts not comprehending a word of the thanksgiving tendered, swaying from the effects of the wine in the hot sun and hiccuping without restraint. Following the ceremony, Tinker and his flying circus met the awful fury of Captain LaCalle.

Peck's bad boys crept back into their squadron commander's good graces with an extraordinary demonstration of aerobatic formation flying. Staged before the same crowd that they had insulted the day before, the Americans performed vertical climbing banks, dives, zooms, diving spirals, loops, and steep chandelles all in tight vee formation. Captain LaCalle accepted the accolades of stunned politicos and awestruck fellow officers alike with counterfeit humility. The Americans' mechanics patronized the ground crews of Spanish patrols whose pilots could not match the Americans' flying acumen. It amazed Tinker that the Republican aviators accepted this condescension good-naturedly and actually praised those Yankees who brought honor to the squadron.

On February 5, LaCalle scheduled a simulated dogfight between the Americans and a squadron of seasoned Russian pilots just back from the

Madrid front. At a prearranged spot, the two sides tangled in mock combat. Tinker succumbed in fifteen minutes, then poor Allison. Dahl, however, scored a technical "kill," tailing his embarrassed Soviet adversary all over the sky. After the contest, victors and vanquished alike piled into a bus headed for Albacete's nightlife.

Great news came in tandem on the morning of February 6. A telegram from Mexico City proclaimed that Allison had fathered a baby boy. No sooner had this bombshell hit than LaCalle ordered the squadron to Guadalajara, about 30 miles northeast of Madrid. A huge Douglas DC-2 transport plane arrived at Albacete to ferry mechanics and luggage, and the pilots flew escort. Crossing the last mountain range before sighting the aerodrome at Guadalajara, LaCalle motioned his pilots to shift into right echelon. The commander's left wingman, Chato Castenedo, swung under LaCalle's machine and simultaneously Leider, who was flying the right wing slot, hit an air pocket and dipped, causing the two fighters to collide in midair. Castenedo's propeller sliced Leider's right tire and gnawed part of his fuselage and lower right wing. In a remarkable feat of airmanship, both Polikarpovs managed to separate. His plane severely damaged, Leider performed a superb "dead-stick," one-wheel landing. Tinker would recall:

> His long experience as a commercial pilot stood him in good stead . . . he finally set her down—left wing low—and when the speed started to fall off, he went into a controlled ground loop to the right. The centrifugal force caused by this maneuver balanced the plane on the left wheel as long as possible, and when the right wheel finally touched the ground it was going so slowly that it just barely went up on its nose before falling back again.

No one doubted Leider's flying ability, not even LaCalle; his instinct for the enemy's jugular, however, was another question yet to be answered.

GUADALAJARA AERODROME

Arriving at Guadalajara, the Americans drooled at the sight of ten new Russian I-16s, sleek-looking monoplanes that reminded Tinker of the U.S. Army's P-26 fighter. Doubtless another mercenary pilot, Englishman Olof de Wet, captured Tinker's infatuation with the Mosca on paper during his own participation in the early defense of Madrid: "How small they look! I am thinking. Like slots in the sky. Like the smallest of flies in a great gray house. Little low-wing monoplanes, undercarriages withdrawn, pilots hidden in their enclosed cockpits, happy there, confident, with 980 horsepower at their fingertips. Who would not be?" LaCalle quipped that the Americans might be allowed to fly such a magnificent airplane after the armistice.

The Madrid-Saragossa railroad ran adjacent to the aerodrome, offering Rebel bombers a combination of tempting strategic targets. Consequently the flats surrounding the airfield reminded Tinker of the crater-pocked surface of the moon. Between the railroad depot station and the base, an assembly plant of the Hispano-Suiza Automobile Company had once stood, now a crumbling ruin. The runway itself was dotted with filled-in bomb craters. A nondescript building at the corner of the complex served as a makeshift pilots club. Luxurious carpets and rich draperies confiscated from a nearby duke's palace made the fieldhouse's warm rooms a shocking contrast to its shabby exterior. It was in the building's assembly hall that the Americans met the Soviet aviators. It amused Tinker that all of the Russians were using Spanish names, and yet their command of the language was as poor as his own. Through an interpreter, the Americans tried shamelessly to ingratiate themselves with their "comrades," thereby hoping to gain access to the new I-16 monoplanes. Unfortunately this stratagem broke down over a question of aeronautical advancements between their respective countries:

Captain Ramon: Have you ever seen planes [I-16s] like those before?

Allison: Segurissimamente. [Why certainly]

Dahl: Hell, yes. [Whitey had actually flown the American P-26 fighter while in the U.S. Army].

Tinker: Si, si.

Captain Ramon (shocked): Do you think that you could fly them?

Dahl: Oh, I flew planes like this about three years ago.

Captain Ramon (astonished): What?

Allison: Yeah, they're a little antiquated, but I suppose we could learn to fly the things again.

Despite the protestations of the Russians, and despite Captain Ramon's appeals to the interpreter, Tinker's crew turned a deaf ear. In fact, the Spanish translator sided with the Americans, insisting that the original model of the Mosca [I-16] had come out of the United States at least four years earlier; he did, however, give the Soviets credit for improving the prototype. The two sides came perilously close to fisticuffs, with the Russian contingent finally stalking away in high dudgeon.

For two solid weeks the LaCalle Squadron sat in the fieldhouse, captives of winter sleet and rain. Looking beyond the airstrip, which was a soggy morass, Tinker could see the looming Sierra Guadarrama mountains. He and the others had been warned that its crest marked the boundary between

Government and Rebel territory should anyone become lost.

Tinker knew that Loyalist pilots felt an abiding dread about going down in enemy territory, and the Air Ministry's foreign volunteer flyers were especially vulnerable. The cruelty of Franco's Moorish troops was legend, and for a mercenary to fall into their hands would mean torture and certain death. Jim Allison petitioned his superiors for sidearms, which Republican flyers had never carried, so that an aviator, if he did crash on the Nationalist side, could reserve a final bullet for himself. Caution dictated, however, that Loyalist airmen perform their fighting over friendly terrain whenever possible.

It was during this bleak period that La Patrulla Americana got better acquainted. Allison monopolized a dilapidated easy chair before the club's fireplace, spinning yarns about his early aerial exploits as a Navy pilot, barnstormer, and bootlegger. Thoughts of his new bride in Mexico City had a mellowing effect on the Texan. Whitey Dahl's florid complexion and extremely blond hair fascinated many of his Spanish compadres. Similarly, his espoused infatuation with his wife in Paris was a source of wonderment to the patrol. As a Southerner, Tinker regarded Leider with grudging admiration. He sat bemused as the New Yorker, an avowed Communist, regaled the squadron on world politics: "I wasn't a member of any party, but I would frequently get into arguments with Ben over the social system down South. He won the arguments. We liked him most for the fact that with no previous military training, he had volunteered for duty in fighting planes." The money off the table, Leider made his fellow flyers feel good about themselves and their service to the Republic. Everybody knew that Leider had refused mercenary pay to fly against the fascists. Even among his squadronmates, however, he was quiet, shy, somewhat lonely. His intense, dark, and rather handsome face was usually grave, his black eyes frequently hard. When Leider became angry, as during one of his political p-ontifications, he had a way of clenching his fists inside his pockets. Despite his religious affiliation, there was something Christlike about him: his sense of altruism, fairness, and faith in humanity served as a beacon to the others.

The flying suits were all the same size and just about right for the Americans; but a five-feet-four Chang Selles was completely lost in his tog, and a collective guffaw arose whenever he appeared in his outfit. Affectionately known as "the runt," Selles was a favorite with everyone, and his excellent knowledge of both Spanish and English made him indispens-able to the group. These "Yanquis" were on good terms with their Spanish flying mates and proudly answered to the nicknames assigned to them. Jim Allison was "Jeem," Leider was "Lando," and Whitey bore the moniker

"Rubio," the Spanish for "blond." Tinker was "Trejo" (pronounced "tray-ho") and also acknowledged the name "Francisco," inherited from the Russians. The Reds considered it more comradely to address one by the first name.

THE PERILS OF SPANISH CUISINE

During this early phase of his tour, the Air Ministry provided Tinker with 200 pesetas for hotel lodging and the food bill, the latter consisting of a midday repast at two o'clock in the afternoon just prior to siesta time. The meal consisted of a fish chowder, a type of ersatz bouillabaisse, and he had it four times out of five. The remainder of Tinker's meals he bought on his own. Spanish currency, though worthless outside the country, still possessed buying power within, and a decent meal could be ordered for 20 cents American. Better still for the young recruit, a bottle of cognac sold for about 35 cents.

The American pilots were not used to so much olive oil in their food. Most of them were reduced to eating nothing but eggs. Of course, eggs were saturated in oil as well, but the Yanks simply held them on their forks until the goo drained away. The mercenaries constantly complained of diarrhea as a result of Spanish cooking. Tinker preferred luncheon fare, which was often served from large wicker baskets right on the runway. These meals consisted of bread with the firmness of concrete, equally hard slabs of ham or slices of goat meat, hardboiled eggs, and two bottles of wine per pilot.

Tinker soon discovered that his adventures in eating were no less challenging off base. Well into his tour of duty, both he and his wingman became lost and were forced to land at an emergency field near the village of Villanueva de la Jara. That evening (April 6) the flyers dined with the local alcalde. Family, guests, and the two pilots gathered in the cooking room of the official's home with its open fire and its huge ceiling in the shape of an inverted funnel.

The mayor's wife and daughter brought in a large pan and a freshly butchered kid. While the older woman cut the goat into small pieces, the girl greased the skillet, coating its sides with garlic, onion, and other seasonings. With this preparation completed, the meat went into the pan. As Tinker, his native squadronmate, and the alcalde talked and sipped wine, his host reached for a knife with one hand and the goat's scrotum with the other without dropping the conversation; he proceeded to extract the testicles, lay them open, wrap them with an unknown material, and place them in the hot ashes under the pan. After a time he removed the sizzling parcel from the fire and awarded one testicle each to Tinker and his comrade. There was nothing left for the guests to do except to eat their appetizers.

With the goat meat fully simmered, the women added vegetables and condiments. Another hour passed, and then the pan was removed from the grill and placed on the floor within reach of all the diners. The alcalde's daughters circled the group dispensing sharp knives and bread—no plates. The Spanish aviator explained to Tinker that the meat and vegetables were speared by each guest and placed on the flat bread held on one's lap. Once placed on the loaf, the main course was devoured with pieces of bread torn from the outer edges. By the time the individual had worked his or her way to the center of the ersatz plate, it was saturated in juice, and this portion of the loaf was eaten as a dessert. The mayor topped off this sumptuous repast with an assortment of local wines.

BAUMLER JOINS KOCH AT LOS ALCAZARES

On the day the LaCalle volunteers left for Alcantarilla, Albert Baumler arrived at Los Alcazares. With his refresher course behind him, Ajax had moved on to La Rabasa Airfield near Alicante. There he suffered through a week with the Nieuport 52, before his introduction to the I-15 at Los Alcazares. Koch and Baumler rekindled their old friendship from San Javier days (December 1936). His health restored, Koch and "the Keed," as he called Ajax, flew jaunts out of Los Alcazares. This happy time ended on February 9, when the two went to Los Llanos Airfield near Albacete, home of the International Brigades. Koch and Baumler were conscripted into a thrown-together squadron to bolster the collapsing Málaga front. The seven Chatos were led by a Russian named Kosokov. Teamed with the Americans were five veteran Soviets, who had survived the dogfights over Madrid during November and December 1936.

Koch and Baumler took part in a mission which marked the end of the famous Escadre Malraux. On this February 11 raid, the Potez bombers left Tabernas bound for Málaga. The Potezs were escorted by Kosokov's I-15s. The Chatos flew high cover for their death-laden charges at 18,000 feet. As this strike force approached Málaga, the formation flew out of the sun. From the sea, three Fiats appeared and pounced upon the bombers. By the time Kosokov's Polikarpovs reached the Potezs, two were in distress. A stricken Fiat spiraled downward, while the other two engaged the I-15s. Koch shot down a second CR 32, and the survivor fled. Returning to

Tabernas, the Chatos overtook the wounded bombers. One tried to land in the sea near Motril. On the flight to base, the squadron overflew the second bomber which crashed in a pasture near Llanos de Dalias, only 30 miles from Tabernas.

JARAMA–TINKER'S BAPTISM AS FIGHTER PILOT

The LaCalle squadron made its combat debut on February 10 with flights over Nationalist territory. Fighting cold drizzle and dense cloud banks, Tinker persevered, his Chato carrying four 25 lb. bombs under its lower wing. LaCalle pinpointed the first targets as gunpowder factories just across the Jarama River about 15 miles southeast of Madrid. Cloaked in the shroud of a 3,000-foot cloud bank, the nimble I-15s sped across the front lines. LaCalle had his pilots in a formation known as a V of Vs, which meant that the biplanes of each patrol were in a V formation and the patrols themselves were flying in V formation on LaCalle's patrol. Diving on their objectives in the same formation, LaCalle's patrol neutralized an anti-aircraft battery between the factories while each wing patrol bombed the installations. Once his bombs had been jettisoned, Tinker utilized the remainder of his almost vertical plunge in strafing hapless factory workers and Rebel troops. Finally flattening out in the dive, he and the others zipped across the Jarama River and eluded enemy pursuits by flying low to the ground through valleys and ravines. That afternoon the squadron hit the same two factories again and machine gunned Insurgent trenches on the return trip. Back at base, the air was blue with La Calle's "admonitions," with the captain's ire directed mainly at the Americans for risking men and machines–both precious commodities–to a well-aimed bullet. That evening, several squadrons of German Junkers 52 bombers repaid Tinker's aerodrome in kind for the earlier raid.

Orders came down on February 11 to bomb and strafe enemy artillery positions directly across the Jarama from Aranjuez. La Patrulla Americana was to return to the airstrip by way of a particular bridge that the Rebels sought to wrest from Government troops. Tinker's memories of the hours before this and other missions would be with him for the remainder of his abbreviated life:

While armorers check bombs and guns, Tinker and fellow pilots gather for instructions. LaCalle gives the orders in his native tongue as the aviators pour over a huge wall map; then the men consult their own flight maps as one Spaniard or another translates the commander's directives to the Americans–a precaution.

Everyone jokes a bit afterwards, then heads for the parked fighters, and above the roar of twenty-odd Cyclone engines, the airmen wish one another "buena suerte." Tinker lingers an extra moment or two among the sweating mechanics. The air blast from his propeller wash revives him, plastering his clothing to his spare frame. The weight of his parachute beneath his bottom affords him a measure of reassurance even as it hinders his access to the Chato's cockpit. Settled at last, Tinker opens the engine without a glance at his instruments, experiencing through repetition and intuition his powerplant's perfect burst to life. His mechanic shouts to him with a grin: "Un centimo malo siempre volvera" ("A bad penny always comes back"). He hunches in his seat for what seems an eternity. Unflattering thoughts about LaCalle creep into his consciousness: "What the hell's the delay—is he waiting for the fascists to set up their antiaérea?" Abruptly, LaCalle pivots his Chato around and raises his gloved hand. The flights trail one another closely on the take-off; then the I-15s form an echelon of Vs and head off at about 1,000 meters. At a designated altitude the formation begins a gradual powerglide descent, and the Polikarpovs transform themselves into a string formation—with the Vs stretched out one behind the other.

Squadron leader LaCalle's patrol started its dive over the batteries with Tinker's wing about 1,600 feet behind. Tinker saw that the anti-aircraft bursts were so thick that one could walk on them, but as the I-15s were doing over 300 miles per hour in a vertical dive, there was no turning back. The next barrage of white puffs framed LaCalle's men almost perfectly before a shell struck his left wingman's gas tank. For an instant Tinker observed in wonder as the Chato exploded in a mushroom cloud of black smoke, leaving behind wing and tail fragments drifting earthwards. Snatched from his reverie by his own perilous situation and having successfully completed his bombing run, Tinker veered away from the flak patterns and headed for home. On his return flight he machine gunned Rebel troops attempting to invest their secondary target—the unnamed bridge—in revenge for the life of José Calderon, LaCalle's best friend and boon companion. When Tinker offered his sympathy to Calderon's Spanish comrades, they merely shrugged and murmured "Esta la guerra." LaCalle and the others brooded for a time, but inured to the butchery all around them in Spain, they soon brightened at the prospects of life's pleasures and adventures.

Tinker saw the native pilots' sense of detachment and fatalism as a natural reaction to war-weariness and a manifestation of the dark side of the Spanish character, yet similar signs of resignation from the civilian population seemed to make him angry. Once on furlough at Valencia's Hotel Ingles, he grew uncomfortable witnessing the destruction of a nearby apartment building, later writing: We watched them searching the debris for bodies—and finding portions of them. . . . Once, when the shattered remains of a small child were brought up, a few of them showed signs of emotion, but the majority of them never so much as moved a muscle of their faces. I can almost see the crowds standing around watching the Little Rock Fire Department dig bodies out of the Albert Pike or the Ben McGhee hotels—though why any enemy with good sense would want to bomb Little Rock, I couldn't say—and philosophically discussing the condition of the remains.

CAMPO X

Campo X was the site of Tinker's new airstrip, a private field 9 miles from Guadalajara. The move necessitated a change in living quarters from the more sumptuous accommodations in Guadalajara's hotel to a private dwelling in the town of Azuqueca, near Campo X. The aerodrome was situated on the country estate of a former count with the nobleman's villa located at one corner of the field. The count's home was ringed by modest dwellings used by his retainers in better days. Now Loyalist militia stayed there to guard the pilots.

In true democratic style, the flyers and their mechanics sat for meals in the count's main dining hall. It amazed Tinker to discover during these gatherings that many of the mechanics were commissioned officers, while a number of the Spanish aviators were NCOs. While in U.S. Army and Navy flying units military rankings were just the reverse, in the Republican Air Force all promotion in both mechanics' and pilots' branches was based on either length of service or deeds of bravery. The Arkansan's own mechanic, Chamorro, held the rank of first lieutenant, while Tinker was only a second lieutenant.

After a few weeks LaCalle informed the mechanics that they were to eat and sleep separately from the pilots and the Russian technical advisors. Although the ground crewmen demonstrated at first, they eventually accepted this elitist gesture with grudging compliance. The commander reasoned that he wanted to corral all of his airmen or technical personnel at a moments' notice, without having to scour the base or nearby Azuqueca. It was the prospect of losing sleep due to late night pilot conferences, however, which settled the matter in the minds of the mechanics.

Tinker's quarters at Campo X airfield were quite luxurious. He resided in a huge octagonal building with large rooms, each of which had windows on the outside of the building and opened into a large central dining room. The ceiling of this central room was the top of the building, with a skylight 10 feet square. The kitchen was just off the banquet room, so that meals were always hot. There were eight large bedrooms on the ground floor for the pilots. The upper rooms accommodated the kitchen staff and the young señoritas who cleaned the building, washed clothes, and otherwise saw to the needs of the pilots. The mechanics stayed in a building adjacent to the Casa de Pilotos. Tinker and Chang Selles enjoyed the female companionship of Maria and Christina respectively, seamstresses who worked in the sewing room there.

As close as two sisters could be, these Madrileños were in their early twenties and well educated for the time. Christina possessed a high school diploma, and Maria finished her sophomore year at the University of Madrid. They had been assigned to the base's sewing room because they were the only women at Campo X who understood the operation of the new American sewing machine with which the seamstress shop was equipped. Their father and two brothers had taken to the barricades in defense of the capital, and a third sibling had already given his life to the Republic.

Aerial bombardments and protracted February rains made life a nightmare at Campo X. During a harrowing raid on his first night at the new airfield, Tinker hit the bottom of a slit trench so hard that he lost two front teeth. Worse still, Chang Selles' refurbished I-15, just back from an Albacete repair station, suffered a direct hit during a raid, thereby grounding him indefinitely. Muddy runway conditions hampered Government fighters in rising to meet the nettlesome bombers.

Beside himself due to the squadron's seeming inability to function either offensively or defensively, LaCalle ordered the squadron back to the base at Guadalajara. There the patrol took on bombs and went aloft once again in quest of Insurgent railroad stations. On February 12, tired and ill-tempered, Tinker and the others happened across an enemy troop train stopped at a depot; after bombing both train and station, the LaCalle squadron returned and gunned down the fascist troops spilling from the disabled railroad cars.

God flew with Tinker during this bloody mission. In the midst of his strafing runs, he felt an unusual vibration throughout the plane. Suspecting that the problem stemmed from his two upper machine guns in the Chato's fuselage, Tinker switched to his twin lower guns below the propeller to complete his deadly work. When he investigated at the field, he discovered that, indeed, his upper machine guns had become unsynchronized and had put a total of sixteen bullet holes through his propeller blades. Had Tinker fired the defective guns several more times, he would have lost a blade, and his radial engine would have shaken itself free of the machine. The shaken pilot mused that he would have been too low to deploy his parachute.

The following morning, Tinker's damaged propeller blades were replaced in time for another bombing sortie. The blades were so out of alignment, however, that the resultant vibration shook off his bombs over a wheat field shortly after takeoff. Though Tinker dressed down his mechanics for their carelessness, the same problem recurred on an afternoon mission. No sooner had he brought his quaking Chato home a second time, than the aerodrome's emergency signal—two red flares—arched over the field. Immediately all of the Russian I-16s soared aloft in the direction of the squadron he had been compelled to abandon. When LaCalle's Escuadrilla and the Moscas returned, Tinker learned that his comrades had stumbled across an enemy patrol and had dogfought the Germans before the I-16s broke off the engagement. The squadron returned intact, and a beaming Ben Leider claimed a Heinkel 51 in the duel.

LEIDER'S CONTROVERSIAL VICTORY

A U.S. Communist Party tract subsequently published Leider's reaction to his feat: "I picked out my man—a Heinkel—and went in after him with the machine guns going. Suddenly I saw water dripping from the Heinkel and knew that I had hit him in the cooling tank. A minute later he was falling in flames. As the Heinkel plunged downward, I saw neither plane nor pilot falling. I saw fascism itself crashing to earth." Leider wrote his folks concerning his kill: " . . . yesterday, the 13th, was my lucky day! I had my first combat and downed my first Heinkel! LaCalle was with me when I got the dog down. I saw water leave his radiator in a streak as he made for his lines. Now, if anything happens [to me], at least I haven't been a liability." Still another account held that Leider scored this victory without firing a shot. This version maintained that he closed on the Heinkel, but did not trip his guns. Instead, the German aviator dropped to treetop level in an attempt to elude his pursuer, brushed a tree with his bottom wing, lost control of the plane, and flipped over into the ground. The I-16s claimed four additional Heinkels, so that night the two squadrons celebrated at a local hotel until LaCalle proclaimed curfew.

Tinker's continuing problems with his badly aligned propeller had put him in a dark mood when he landed at Campo X on February 14. Still in his Chato's cockpit, he reported his ship's condition to LaCalle and then proceeded to taxi over to his patrol's designated parking area. Several huge ponds of water were between Tinker and his destination; aggravated by his pursuit's poor performance, he decided to taxi right through the largest of these lagoons instead of going around it. Halfway through this morass, his

Polikarpov bogged down completely, leaving its pilot in a state of helplessness.

LaCalle was in a rage. "Trejo,' he bellowed, "you damned fool, why didn't you go around that laguna?" As Tinker's countrymen raced up to water's edge, LaCalle collared Chang Selles and ordered him to interpret. Cornered and without the protection of his poor Spanish, "Trejo' responded: "Why I thought this was as good a place to taxi as going around. What's wrong with that?" "What's wrong with that," screamed LaCalle. "You idiot, what kind of damn flying training did you have in the United States?"

At that instant, divine inspiration came to Tinker: "I was trained at the Navy flying school and, as you can see, I am merely a trifle absent-minded." The picture of Tinker seated in his I-15, fuselage-deep in water, struck the American gallery as hilarious. LaCalle stalked away cursing his fate.

Tinker's running squabble with the mechanics over his engine's vibration lasted several more days until he himself located the problem: dirt between the propeller hub and its shaft. No sooner had this mechanical difficulty been solved than one of a political nature surfaced. Tinker's mechanic, Chamorro, was a Communist. Allison's and Selles' mechanics were Anarchists. Dahl's man was a Socialist. All four got into a violent political altercation, which ended with the declaration by the fuming Anarchists that from henceforth they were not going to assist each other or the other two mechanics. "Rubio's" Socialist crewman adopted the same position. Since teamwork among the mechanics was required to keep the patrol in the air, La Patrulla Americana faced a real dilemma. The three pilots huddled. Then they strolled over to Tinker's I-15, initiated a conversation, and pretended to get into an argument. When their histrionics reached the shouting stage, the mechanics edged closer, only to see their respective pilots march off in different directions. Chamorro was delegated to ask Chang Selles the problem. The diminutive aviator solemnly explained that the conflict had arisen over party politics back in the United States. What concerned Selles (tongue-in-cheek) were the defiant assertions that the trio would never again come to one another's aid, either in the air or on the ground. The ground crew could not believe their ears. Most assuredly lives would be lost and the Yanquis' beautiful formation flying would be a thing of the past. Within minutes, Chamorro confronted his boss with the mechanics' supplication for unity among the flyers. A grudging Tinker conceded, but only after exacting the same concession from the mechanics. A bemused Tinker would subsequently write of this comic opera: "They saw the moral of our false argument and went to work on my plane at once. After that, we never did have any more trouble, as far as the upkeep of our planes was concerned."

That afternoon (February 16), over the Jarama River south of Madrid, the squadron happened across six trimotored Junker 52 bombers. No sooner had the group prepared to attack the formation than six more bombers materialized, offering the prospect of an aerial massacre. From experience, Tinker knew that the lumbering Junkers had a blind spot forward due to the machine's central engine; therefore, the I-15s and I-16s attacked head on.

TINKER'S DRILL ON FLAMING FASCIST BOMBERS

For Tinker and the rest of the patrol, the whole business of approaching fascist bombers amounted to a science. Most Nationalist bombers could not fire straight up. Therefore, all La Patrulla Americana fighters needed was a 50-degree angle, or less, above the bomber. Tinker's Chato would circle or S-climb to about 3,000 feet slightly ahead of and above the bomber formation. A half roll brought him into a vertical dive, but slightly over on the plane's back. By this time, the fighter had the bomber's range, it was beyond the forward gunner's elevation as a result of its momentum, and his pursuit commanded a clean sweep of the cockpit, top fuselage, and tail assembly of the bomber. The telescopic sight gave Tinker a good close-up, and the concentric rings helped in deflection allowance. The most effective range in the dive was about 1,500 feet. When within 800–500 feet of the target, Tinker pulled out at a 25–30 degree angle and to the side and slipped as much as possible. Thus only the guns from one side of the bomber could lay a bead on him, and at his diving speed he was never hit. Before the enemy bomber could raise its nose or tail in order to bring its gunners into action, the lumbering giant was usually already in flames. By slipping after the attack, Tinker gave the Rebel gunners double range, deflection, and trajectory trouble, any of which proved sufficient to guarantee his escape.

Of course, there were always variations on a central theme of attack. While the slow Junker 52s called for a frontal charge, the speedy Dornier Do 17s, or "Flying Pencils," required a rear-on attack. Once behind this bimotored Nazi bomber, Tinker hid behind the ship's twin rudders and sprayed the rear gunner with lead. Once he had silenced this defender, prospects were good as the machine was defenseless from the rear. During these assaults, Tinker's huge Cyclone engine deflected the rear gunner's field of fire until his comrades could kill him. On this particular February afternoon, however, Ju 52s were on the menu, and La Patrulla Americana's approach was working all too well:

As we followed LaCalle around the left turn and into the dive, we saw heading straight for us, six more Junkers. These, being nearer, looked even larger and more impressive than the first six. So each of us—eleven in all—went down the alley, one after the other, holding down all four machine-gun trips throughout the dive. When each man got as close to the Junkers as he could without crashing into them, he would execute a half-roll and dive away from them. As I pulled out at the bottom of my first dive, I looked back and saw the leading Junker slowly turning over, and as it turned I saw the reason why. The pilot's cockpit was an inferno of flames. It turned over completely and then plummeted to the ground, bombs and all, where it crashed with a terrific explosion.

LaCalle's patrols circled around in front of the 52s again and commenced another strafing run. A second Junker belched black smoke from its nose engine and went down into a shallow dive. The stricken bomber crashed in the middle of the Jarama River, its hapless crew offering perfect targets to Republican militiamen on the banks. Not until he returned to the aerodrome did Tinker learn that Soviet-piloted I-16s had provided LaCalle's flyers the luxury of a turkey-shoot, having first downed a number of Heinkel fighter escorts.

On February 17 the squadron sighted two patrols of Italian Fiats on the Jarama front; despite giving chase, the CR 32s refused to engage LaCalle's Chatos. This act of perceived cowardice irritated Tinker, who had never tangled with a Fiat, which had been limited to southern Spain. He and his cohorts had come to regard the Heinkels as relatively easy pickings and they hankered for a true aerial contest with Rebel pilots. In time, Tinker displayed contempt for Mussolini's aviators, although he had been told that the Republic's brave volunteers of the "Garibaldi Battalion" were not afraid to fight. This contradiction perplexed him, and on more than one occasion he was heard to mutter, "If there had been German pilots in those Fiat fighters there would have been an entirely different story after any of our dogfights."

RADIO DAYS

That evening an ongoing international dispute over the flyers' house radio resulted in a total victory for the Americans. The bickering stemmed from the fact that the Spanish pilots always tuned in the Spanish stations, the Russian aviators selected the Russian stations, and Tinker's group competed for English or American stations. La Patrulla Americana devised a scheme to block the competition by forming a semicircle of chairs around the shortwave receiver. Of course, the other Spanish pilots adopted this tactic and, because they greatly outnumbered their foreign comrades, successfully monopolized the radio. Tinker countered by attaching a rubber suction head to the end of a cue stick. Armed with this instrument, he could easily reach over the human blockade and manipulate the control buttons of the shortwave set. LaCalle's men were delighted by Tinker's ingenuity and awarded him all stations gotten in this manner. All nationalities, however, enjoyed listening to the entertaining broadcasts of Franco's General Queipo de Llano, head of the Rebel South Army, who had become popular for his propaganda via radio. Whenever he referred to Republican aviators as "bicycle pilots," his appreciative listeners roared their approval.

For both sides of the air war, the battle of the Jarama and its defining aerial battle of February 18 represented a protracted and sweeping chronological account, a militarily controversial subject, and a convoluted political history. Franco meant to envelope Madrid with the Army of Africa and the North Army east of the capital between Guadalajara and Alcalá de Henares. A vicious battle raged through most of January; three Red brigades dissolved, and the vaunted Thaelmann Battalion (11th International Brigade) ceased to exist. Despite Rebel advances on the Corunna road, subsequent Loyalist counterattacks gained much of the lost territory back. Madrid had survived the immediate threat of fascist encirclement.

As General Queipo de Llano's South Army entered Málaga in early February, however, fighting erupted again on the Madrid front. Since the Insurgents left pincer of encirclement had stalled on the Corunna road, Franco's attention focused on the right prong, which was to breach the Republican front south of the Jarama River. He wanted this drive to cut the Valencia road and unite, near Alcalá de Henares, with the North Army pushing southwest from north of Brihuega. The success of this campaign hinged on the abrogation of communications between Madrid and Valencia. The Nationalists' edge in artillery was more than matched by the Government's Soviet aircraft.

As early as February 7, an Insurgent brigade reached the confluence of the Jarama and Manzanares rivers and brought the Valencia road under fire. Bad weather, however, conspired to halt all advancement, and by dusk on February 12 the fascist push had been contained. The following day, International volunteers and Soviet tanks drove the Nationalists back to the Jarama. By February 17 the Loyalists had counterattacked with an army corps under unified command. This huge force struck between La Marañosa and Cerro de los Angeles. The Republican Madrid Corps made ground and took the Pingarrón Heights on February 19, but it was driven back by the

Moroccans at great cost. This sector changed hands several times with a horrifying loss of life.

In the air, General Vincenzo Velardi, commander-in-chief of the Aviazione Legionaria, decreed that Fiats were not to penetrate enemy territory, and now Maggiore Tarscisco Fagnani meant to continue observance of this long-standing order. The Spanish Nationalist air chief, General Alfredo Kindelán, saw Velardi's mandate as an opportunity to force the Italians to equip all native pursuit units with Fiats. Kindelán instructed Morato to transfer the Blue Patrol to the Jarama front and, at the first opportunity, attack Republican planes over their own territory.

THE AERIAL CLASH OF FEBRUARY 18

On the morning of February 18, two Spanish Nationalist Romeo Ro 37 light bombers took off, followed by three Ju 52s, and escorted by Morato's Blue Patrol and the Italian Fiat group of 24 aircraft. When this attack formation reached the front lines, the Fiats veered so that they were patrolling parallel to the front, while the deadly Chatos waited on the other side. The Rebel bombers passed into enemy territory and were beset immediately. Morato abandoned the Fiat group and, trailed by Blue Patrol comrades Salvador and Bermudez de Castro, propelled himself into the fray. The Italians showed indecision until the veteran, Captain Guido Nobili, quit the defensive formation and flew to the Spaniards' aid. Within seconds, collective shame incited the entire group into action. Frank Tinker viewed this contest through a different lens, however, even as to the number and type of enemy fighters.

On the morning of February 18, the LaCalle squadron engaged 85 Heinkel 51s (Fiats) over the front. Immediately the Escuadrilla de LaCalle went into a tight horizontal circle—or Lufbery formation—and awaited the enemy. The first 51s (Fiats) fired randomly at the Chatos as they dived past the squadron's defensive pattern. Unwilling to challenge the Government fighters, the remainder of the German (Italian) pilots followed suit, executing a single strafing pass, and then flying lazily below the I-15s in hopes of enticing a few green Loyalist aviators away from LaCalle's fold.

THE DEATH OF BEN LEIDER

Poor Ben Leider took the bait and paid with his life. He started down after one of the easy-looking targets, only to attract three Heinkels (Fiats) on his tail. As Tinker peered over his shoulder during the swirling melee of planes, he saw Leider's Chato shudder as the German (Italian) biplanes flashed past. Then the Arkansan's heart sank as he noticed Leider veer toward friendly territory in a shallow dive. Twice this Jewish idealist tried to land his craft in a small field before slamming into the side of a hill. Tinker sensed that his comrade would not walk away from the smoking debris.

Evidence from the crash site gave Leider's fellow pilots a clue as to his final seconds on earth. During the dogfight, three rounds penetrated his cockpit, one passing through his leg. Instinctively he loosened his seat belt and harness. As Leider prepared to bail out, he had second thoughts about giving up his Chato, so he decided to attempt to set down his plane. His loss of blood caused him to faint at the controls.

LaCalle's version of Leider's end differed markedly from Tinker's perspective. As Leider dived, breaking away from the Lufbery circle to flame a Heinkel circling below, an He 51 (Fiat) locked on his tail. LaCalle pulled behind Leider's pursuer and frightened him away with his machine guns. Repeatedly LaCalle then tried to herd Ben's intended victim back away from Rebel lines so that the American could down the enemy fighter. LaCalle wanted Leider to destroy the Heinkel (Fiat) as a morale boost for the squadron and to appease Leider's Communist backers. When the fascist made a third attempt to cross his lines, LaCalle shot him down. Irritated by the turn of events and Leider's seeming inability to shoot down his adversary, the Spanish commander signaled Leider to head for home. During the flight back to base, Leider flew just behind the squadron leader's wing. Halfway there, LaCalle glanced around only to discover Leider gone. Having landed, he learned that no one knew of the American's whereabouts: his comrades saw him rejoin their homebound group and never again. There was no other news until Leider's Chato was located.

Gene Finick was enjoying a hot soak in an American bathtub at an abandoned palace outside Albacete when word came of Leider's death. The news preyed on his mind all day and into the night: "That night I tossed around repeatedly seeing the face of the remorseful Leider, who had nearly cried the last time I had seen him; at that occasion he was upbraiding himself for washing out the landing gear of one of our early few bombers in making a landing. When I returned to the base and checked my ship for flight I was determined that several of the enemy were going the same way Ben Leider went." Constancia de la Mora, wife of Loyalist Air Force chief Hidalgo de Cisneros, recalled Leider: "So many men we met grew into our hearts and then one day were reported dead. Ben Leider, a young American pilot whom Ignacio admired for his ability and heroism—I met him once with Ignacio. We talked, we would have been friends. And then he was killed."

WHITEY DAHL GOES DOWN

During the February 18 engagement, Tinker also watched in disbelief as the more seasoned Allison and Dahl followed Leider down after the Nationalist fighters. The Texan shot down his intended victim before three Heinkels (Fiats) reached him. Allison's I-15 gave a jerk, then it executed a perfect Immelmann and headed back to base. Dahl prepared to trip his guns on a careless adversary when he noticed the same three Heinkels (Fiats) flash past. Almost simultaneously, he became aware that his machine was not answering the controls. A glance back revealed the answer why: the entire tail of his Chato had been shot away. Watching his friend float down beneath the billows of his parachute, Tinker worried about how "Rubio" would fare on the ground. Still, he maintained his position in the Lufbery circle despite strafing passes from enemy fighters. In the nick of time, another squadron of I-15s appeared piloted by Russian volunteers. Fighting their way through the curtain of Heinkels (Fiats), the Soviets joined LaCalle's men in the wheel formation until the groups were rescued by a third squadron of Moscas (I-16s). The tally from this brief encounter was seven Heinkels (Fiats) and two Chatos downed.

That evening the collective spirits of the flyers hit bottom, and the consumption of alcoholic spirits peaked in the pilots' house. LaCalle's patrol returned minus one plane, the American patrol returned minus two planes, and the third patrol arrived intact. The missing men included, of course, Leider, Allison, and Dahl. It haunted Tinker that he was the only American to return from that awful sortie:

> When Chang and I landed and taxied in to the part of the field occupied by the American patrol, I realized, for the first time, just how our mechanics felt about us Americans. Jim's mechanic, Barca, and Whitey's mechanic, Juanos, evidently saw by the looks on our faces, that something out of the ordinary had happened. Juanos, the Socialist, was actually in tears, while Barca, the hitherto rough-and-ready machinist, had a look on his face that I never want to see again . . . to see a huge, broken-nosed ruffian trying, unsuccessfully, to control his emotions, was almost as bad as seeing Jim, Ben and Whitey shot down.

It was at that moment that Tinker truly grasped the worth of the American flyers to the Republican cause and the depth of his countrymen's commitment to the survival of the Republic. The great unspoken question among airmen and mechanics alike was the same: "How would the Escuadrilla LaCalle fare without its moral and political compass, Ben Leider?"

That same day, Koch's group was headed home for Alcalá de Henares following action over the Jarama River. No sooner had they landed than the squadron was airborne again, this time to confront the enemy over the Madrid front. In this huge aerial battle, fighting alongside the LaCalle squadron and his former comrades, six Fiats went down including "Tiny" Koch's second victim and four Ju 52 bombers in the bargain. The Kosokov outfit flew two more combat missions that day before the sun went down.

LaCalle parked his staff car in the middle of the field the following day with a case of beer in the back seat. After each member of his squadron had guzzled several bottles, LaCalle chastised his men, especially the Americans (Tinker), for breaking formation during the engagement of February 18. His lengthy harangue in the broiling sun evolved into a discourse on the tactics of modern aerial warfare and concluded with a pep talk on the glory of dying for the Cause. Before dismissal, each pilot drew an additional beer.

Morato's Blue Patrol and the Fiat group claimed eight Red machines destroyed to one of their own. For his part in the February 18 engagement, the Spanish ace would receive fascist Spain's highest military decoration. General Kindelán also scored a victory, and the first all-Spanish Fiat escuadrilla, I-E-3, was created with six fighters on March 30, 1937. Soon after Jarama, Commander Tarscisco Fagnani was relieved of duty and returned to Italy. His successors were by their aggressiveness and example, able to erase the reputation for timidity earned by the Italian flyers under Fagnani's tour.

Brooding over the dead and missing was suspended right after the noon meal when red flares sent the patrols aloft. Directly above the Jarama River, the squadron cut short a surprise raid by Rebel Ju 52 bombers from Getafe, an enemy airfield south of Madrid. On spotting the Republican fighters, pilots of the lumbering trimotors wheeled about and headed for their lines and sanctuary. La Escuadrilla de LaCalle dived for the ground as though its commander planned to return to base. As soon as the wily LaCalle neared the deck, however, he led his patrols through valleys well out of sight of the front lines. Once completely obscured, he then backtracked by way of another series of gorges until he again reached the Jarama River. Finally at the destination, the patrols zoomed skyward in hopes of surprising the Junkers bombers returning for another raid on Government targets. This hide-and-seek game continued at length, and twice the bombers were intercepted, only to evaporate in cloud banks.

ALLISON AND DAHL ARE RECOVERED

During the evening mess, Tinker and company received word that Allison and Dahl had survived the previous day's contest; Leider, however, had perished in his crash landing after having been wounded. On the afternoon of February 19, three carloads of boisterous airmen and mechanics dashed over to Alcalá, a nearby aerodrome, where they found Allison recovering from a serious leg wound. Spokesman Tinker plied the patient with cigarettes and cognac before returning to base, where everyone found a grinning Whitey Dahl awaiting them. Dahl lost no time in providing his squadronmates with the particulars of his harrowing adventure once on the ground:

> I was taken to the commander of the Loyalist garrison there [San Martin de la Vega], and I almost fell over when I saw that it was commanded by a woman—a Captain Dolores Something-or-Other. Whoever she was, she certainly had her men well in hand. They really snapped when she spoke. She had a phone call put through to Madrid and they got me a straight-through connection to here. . . . I couldn't get away then on account of a shortage of transportation, but I didn't mind at all.
>
> She took me over to one of the lookout posts and let me take a look at the Fascists walking around over in San Martin [across the river]. They seemed to me to be within rifle range, so I asked her why they didn't crack down on them. She gave me the astonishing reply that they never fired upon each other during the siesta period. . . .
>
> That's about all there was to it. A few hours later I got word that a car from Madrid was waiting for me in front of garrison headquarters, and in a couple of hours I was in Madrid. Then this morning I was sent to Alcalá, where I gave the group commander a statement about the affair. I hung around the flying field over there all afternoon, and they finally managed to spare a car for me to make the trip over here. Nothing to it. Oh, yes, I forgot to mention that Captain Dolores traded pistols with me before I left the garrison. She wanted something to remember me by. Don't tell my wife about it, though.

The dawn brought honor to LaCalle's squadron on February 20. His four patrols would herald the beginning of the Government's counterattack on the Jarama front. For days, the Nationalists had been massing in this sector. The fascist objective was to cut the road between Madrid and Valencia, and the Rebels had succeeded in driving a salient across the river which threatened to accomplish that end. By the 20th, however, the Republicans had concentrated enough reinforcements in this area to effect a counterattack. LaCalle's flyers began bombing and machine gunning artillery emplacements in the salient. The action resulted in a massacre as the Rebels were caught either in the midst of lunch or an afternoon siesta by the strafing I-15s. No sooner had LaCalle's last plane taken its deadly pass than the Soviets resumed the killing, while two Mosca squadrons presided over the slaughter from high above. The wretched Nationalist troops ran pell-mell for the Jarama River abandoning the salient to the Loyalist forces.

The squadron had scarcely touched down when it was airborne again, this time to challenge German bombers. As LaCalle threw the Chatos into left echelon in preparation for an attack on the Junkers, the fascist bombers turned so that all of their machine guns would be trained on the attacking Red biplanes.

> I was in so close to Whitey that I was almost firing in formation with him. We each fired for about thirty seconds—until we were about a hundred yards from the Junkers—and then went into our half-rolls and dove away; noting as we did so, that one of them was dropping out of the formation. As we pulled up into formation again, though, we could see one of our own biplanes headed for the ground in a crazy flat spin. As we watched, it crashed into the ground. (Tinker)

As the Chatos came round for a second pass, the Junkers full throttled and sped across the invisible line that divided armies and ideologies. The crippled bomber, however, glided across the Jarama and crash-landed, a "kill" confirmed by friendly ground observers. The biplanes then climbed to where the I-16s were mastering the antiquated Heinkels. Condor Legion pilots found themselves in immediate peril, for while the He 51 could outdive the Chatos, they were nevertheless unable to outdive the Russian monoplanes. Conversely the Germans knew that their Heinkels could climb faster than the I-16s but were no match for the I-15 biplanes. Therefore, with no more Rebel bombers left to escort and with a deadly union of enemy Polikarpovs in the offing in an already unequal dogfight, the Heinkels fled. Adolf Hitler's expatriated Luftwaffe left seven of its company on an ethereal field of battle that afternoon. Evening assembly brought the sad news that the squadron's deputy leader, Luis Bercial, perished in the exchange, shot down by the Italian ace Guido Nobili. His loss left LaCalle with only eight of the original twelve members of the squadron, José Calderon, Leider, and Berthial having been killed and Allison so severely wounded as to be lost for an extended period. In reprisal for the day's successes, waves of Ju 52s pounded the Henares River valley— and Tinker's base—from 9:30 p.m. until past midnight. At sunset on February 21, LaCalle bombed and strafed the few remaining Rebels on the Republican side of the Jarama River, his flyers spraying the tiny enclave with 80,000 rounds of ammunition.

From February 24 to March 5, torrential rains grounded the squadron. During these gray days, the aviators assembled in the pilots' house to mess, socialize, and trade gossip. These gatherings took on the aspect of an international conclave; it was during one such meal that several Soviet pilots brought Tinker news of old comrades. It seemed that Al Baumler and Charlie Koch, whom Tinker had known at Manises, were scheduled to transfer to LaCalle's outfit. Both men had been flying with the Russians on the Málaga front prior to reassignment. Of the two airmen, it was Baumler who stood out in Tinker's memory as a daring flyer blessed with great predatory instincts.

MALRAUX'S AMERICAN TOUR

Across the Atlantic Ocean, André Malraux's liner docked in New York City on February 24 amid great fanfare. Many adoring New Yorkers thronged the pier to glimpse the warrior-intellectual whose private air force helped to save the Republic in its darkest hour. Malraux had crossed the sea to tout the Republican cause and to raise money to purchase ambulances and medical supplies. In another capacity, he had come as the titular head of the Alliance of Anti-Fascist Intellectuals, hoping to swell its membership through American recruitment. At every turn, interrogators wanted to know about his role in the international air force. Invariably, Malraux discussed the mercenaries who flocked to Spain.

> We had many freaks [he admitted]. The first freaks were the tragic kind—men who had not flown since the World War, but who claimed to be good aviators. Some were given good planes, but they broke them up immediately, killing themselves. We had an American who pestered the war offices for days trying to put across an idea he had for a trotting bomb. He said his bomb would trot into enemy territory and then explode.

The writer raised some funds, reduced his audiences to tears with stories filled with bravery and pathos, but seemed incapable of shaking the Roosevelt administration, which alone could provide the food, weapons, and aircraft required to save the Republic. Every government official in

Washington rebuffed him, and there were mutterings about revoking his entry permit.

Malraux appeared at three separate fund raisers in Hollywood, lectured before a group of writers at Princeton, attended a dinner given in his honor by *The Nation*, and scheduled numerous interviews. Frequently his inspirational talks contained long passages from *Man's Hope*, which he was still writing. The idealist returned to Spain, sadder but wiser, and, in the summer of 1937, he attended the second International Congress of Writers in Madrid. The Republic feted the honored guests, gave them expensive remembrances, and praised their efforts; after all, they kept the faith with the Cause. Awash in this good feeling, Malraux nevertheless realized that it would take more than personal steadfastness to save the Republican cause.

5

AMERICAN PALADINS IN ACTION

> Chang's [Selles] plane was the one shot up in our patrol—it had thirty-five or forty bullet holes in it. . . . The funny thing about it was that he thought someone in the third patrol had been shooting at him; he had not seen the Fiats at all.
>
> Tinker at Guadalajara

DIVERSIONS AT CAMPO X

During inclement weather, there were many diversions at Campo X to pass the time, and for Tinker and Dahl looting was high on the list. Happening across a storage attic in the former owner's estate house, the two discovered a treasure trove. Tinker liberated a dueling sword, "three rather aged paintings," a collection of spurs, and a leather shepherd's pouch. Dahl's selections were about as random. Chang Selles and Tinker also spent a lot of time with the base's seamstresses, Christina and Maria. These bachelors liked to wait until their girlfriends finished work, and the four of them would walk to nearby Azuqueca and back. Occasionally, however, the couples went for rides along the Madrid-Guadalajara highway, leaving Whitey, the faithful spouse, and the base chauffeur, to walk to town in each other's company. For more intimate moments together, Tinker and Maria passed the nights in the base's empty *refugios*, or bomb shelters.

On February 25, 1937, Dahl, Selles, and Tinker motored to Madrid on leave, stopping briefly at Alcalá's infirmary to see Allison on the eve of his medical discharge. The Texan's condition had worsened, according to Orrin

Bell, who had visited him on a separate occasion. "Do you know what that so-and-so did?" Tex moaned. "He took a piece of gauze, soaked it in iodine, and passed it through the bullet hole and drew it back and forth like a shoeblack polishing your shoes. Then he sewed it up." "Sewed it up?" Bell repeated. "Sewed up both holes? How does the wound drain?" "It don't. Look." Allison's leg had swollen and turned gray. As soon as an attending intern suggested the possibility of an amputation, Allison reached for his crutches and hobbled out of the field hospital. Once on a train for Barcelona, he transferred to the American Hospital in Neuilly, where the doctors saved his leg. Allison left for home in March.

From Alcalá, the three pilots proceeded to the capital, where they encountered innumerable barricades and annoying security checks on every thoroughfare. Once past the suburbs, the airmen discovered a city devoted to gaiety and seemingly unaffected by the war. The mercenaries dodged clanging streetcars and relished the noisy nightlife, sampling every bar along the way to their destination, which was the Hotel Florida. By the time they reached the hotel, the threesome had acquired numerous bottles of champagne. Dahl agreed to carry the magnums while Tinker arranged for rooms. Once on the elevator, Dahl could not push the buttons to go up or down as his arms were full of champagne. Finally, a burly stranger with a mustache appeared and asked Whitey the reason why he would not activate the lift. Dahl retorted "why the hell didn't he," since it was clear that his own arms were full of spirits. Ernest Hemingway did the honors.

> We got two rooms up on the seventh floor, and just outside of Whitey's room was a huge hole in the corridor floor. The lady in charge of that floor explained that it was only a shell hole, and showed us where it had entered the building through the wall at the end of the corridor. After that we enjoyed the first hot baths we had since leaving Valencia. We lay around in the tubs for about an hour before getting dressed and going down to the tea room, where we bribed one of the waiters to bring us champagne glasses and a bucket of ice. After polishing off a couple of the bottles of champagne we'd picked up we climbed into our car and motored back to Azuqueca, feeling that it wasn't such a bad war after all. (Tinker)

Following their furlough in Madrid, Tinker and Dahl were placed on report for returning to base after curfew and in a state of intoxication. On March 2, Tinker tried to evade his grounding sentence by informing LaCalle that he suffered from toothache—two molars in his lower left jaw. His Spanish commander dispatched the aerodrome chief and Tinker to a Madrid dentist forthwith. The dentist first huddled with the chief, then ushered Tinker into his office; before the Arkansan could explain the situation, he pulled two perfectly good molars:

> On the way back to the field the chief told me that I was to go back to the dentist's office in about two weeks so that he could take plaster casts and start work on a lower plate for me. As I . . . lost my two replaceable lower front teeth during the first bombardment of the field [Campo X] . . . my little trick didn't turn out so badly after all. It would at least result in my being relieved of the embarrassment of going around with a couple of front teeth missing—and at a cost of only two molars!

On March 3, La Escuadrilla LaCalle's first replacement flyer arrived at Campo X. He was introduced simply as Velasco, a tall, dark-haired Spaniard whose "over-the-top" demeanor concerned Tinker. Since no Chato was made available to him right away, Velasco incurred the wrath of his s-quadronmates by trying to crawl into their planes parked around the base. Traditionally, pilots bristle when anyone other than themselves or their mechanics handle their craft, and La Calle's flyers were no exception. The last straw came when Velasco was seen examining the wreckage of Leider's, Dahl's, and Berthial's fighters, which had been transported from the front and left on base for salvage. It occurred to Tinker that perhaps the Spaniard meant to build his own plane. "That fellow came up here to fight," prodded Whitey. Chang Selles confided that the stranger had been in the Republican Air Force before the civil war, but that he had been committed to a mental facility for observation. With this bit of news under his flying cap, Tinker felt more depressed than usual.

The Government's final assault on February 27 was the climax of the battle of the Jarama. From 1,000 feet above enemy positions, gunner Gene Finick's Rasante dived on Rebel troop concentrations and manned trenches. In groups of threes and about 400 meters above their targets, each groundstrafer or Sturmovik opened its motors and commenced firing 2,000 rounds from each of its four downward-pointing PV-1 machine guns. Due to this withering fire, the Insurgents were compelled to stop and entrench. The Nationalists had taken approximately 150 square miles and remained across the Jarama, but Madrid endured and the capital remained connected to Valencia.

THE BATTLE OF GUADALAJARA

Spain's traditional air war of bombing raids and dogfights took a nasty turn in March with the introduction of ground strafing on an extraordinary scale. The prospect of huge Italian infantry units necessitated the employment of this aerial tactic, as neither Republican militia nor volunteer International Brigades could contend with these massive columns alone. The Rebel assault on Guadalajara (a provincial capital northeast of Madrid) numbered 50,000 troops divided between Spanish and Italian commands. The core of the offensive consisted of 30,000 of Mussolini's finest in four divisions: the Black Shirts, the Black Flames, the Black Arrows, and the Littorio Divisions on the left flank of the advance, led by General Mario Roatta. These fearsome divisional titles aside, this force lacked training and battlefield experience, and it suffered from low morale. The columns included 250 tanks and 180 mobile field guns together with approximately seventy trucks per battalion. The Nationalists enjoyed an air umbrella of 50 fighters, but monsoonlike weather kept them at base. Republican pursuits were located at fields circling the battle site; the superior drainage of these airstrips—largely hard-surfaced—helped the Loyalists establish air superiority, while the Insurgents, suffering from the disadvantage of distance, had to operate from natural runways that flooded and were built on high plateaus shrouded in fog and mist.

On March 8, LaCalle received intelligence that the Nationalists had started a drive on the front to the north, the Guadalajara front. Headquarters confirmed that Loyalist infantry had offered stiff resistance, but grudgingly retreated before Italian armor. As the enemy advance extended to March 9 on the Madrid-Saragossa highway, three small towns fell to the fascists. Fortunately, heavy rains produced arterial quagmires and washed out bridges, which slowed the Italian offensive to a crawl. The columns' spearhead continued on for four additional miles, but without logistical reserves, it stalled and retreated. By March 10, the Black Flames and the Black Arrows had seized Brihuega, with the Littorio Division trailing these columns as a reserve. Later in the day, the Black Flames collided with the Loyalists' Garibaldi Battalion. Brihuega's proximity to Guadalajara, only 15 miles away, shocked LaCalle's flyers and cast a pall at the supper mess.

Dawn brought Dahl orders from LaCalle to fly reconnaissance. Whitey's flight confirmed a resumption of the Italian advance. His "one-pass" armed reconnaissance sortie also revealed that the fascist columns were deficient in anti-aircraft protection and beset with flooded and soggy terrain. No sooner had the bombs been loaded under each Chato's lower wing than the visibility dropped to zero. March 11 offered the Americans another dismal aerial opportunity as torrential rains raked the pilots' house with staccato barrages. Unwilling to forestall an attack any longer, LaCalle ordered Tinker and company to trade the warmth of their assembly hall for a wet cockpit and the prospect of heading into a bone-chilling wind.

Cruising above low cloud banks, Tinker's patrol surveyed the Guadalajara front in search of targets. A chance break in the overcast afforded them the opportunity to dive below the ceiling, sight their objective, release their bombs at 600 feet, and begin strafing the milling Italian soldiers. Days of continuous rain had flooded the enemy's trenches and foxholes, so the fascists were innocent of cover. They died where they stood, crouching or running, without the benefit of anti-aircraft protection, cut down by the American's withering fire. Tinker was contemptuous of their random gestures of defiance with sidearms and rifles, and yet he could not squelch feelings of respect and pity for these doomed men.

Stalled Rebel motor units and armor on the Guadalajara highway offered tempting targets, so Tinker's squadron returned to base, collected more bombs, and took off again. This time, however, the LaCalle squadron flew straight into a dangerous thunderstorm; after several near midair collisions, Dahl and Tinker lost contact with their compatriots and landed at Albacete. Once on the ground, the pair met General Yacob Schmouskievich (General Douglas). Whitey and Tinker whiled away the evening renewing old friendships with their Soviet friends from the Alcalá airstrip. Early the next morning, General Douglas and several other Russian pilots escorted their American guests back to Guadalajara. Scarcely had the men landed than their Chatos were armed for another raid. Tinker's orders were to escort Republican bombers during a sortie, and then dive-bomb and machine gun targets-of-choice on the return leg of the mission.

One-hundred-and-forty planes launched against Il Duce's volunteers. The Red Wings strafed the Black Shirts, cutting down regimental commander Alberta Liuzzi. Thirty Loyalist R-Z groundstrafer biplanes raked and bombed the Black Arrows, dispensing wholesale death, including the demise of Roatta's chief-of-staff, Colonel Emilio Faldella. The Chatos were supported by Moscas freed from high air cover. A total of 492 bombs and 200,000 rounds made the difference, together with Russian General Dimitri Pavlov's armor attack on Italian positions. The town of Trijueque was retaken by Republican infantry, and the Garibaldi Battalion overcame the Black Flames.

La Patrulla Americana rendezvoused with the lumbering Potez 54s at 6,500 feet and accompanied them across the front lines. Down below, Tinker noticed that a great battle neared its climax. He saw Italian infantry trying to move a stalled convoy along in the mud. Needless to say, the enemy troops scurried to the safety of the highway's shoulders as the bombers began their attack. The concussion of the dropped explosives sent trucks whirling in the air. The Chatos added to the confusion with repeated strafing passes. Hopes for an orderly retreat vanished with the obliteration of a crossroad northwest of Brihuega, and the eastern and central Italian advances, framed by muddy fields and impassable highways to the rear, simply absorbed the aerial punishment.

Each V formation of the bomb-laden Chato group had been assigned a section of the troop-clogged highway; and as the I-15s descended and jettisoned their concussive and fragmentation payloads in a second pass, a rolling tide of fire enveloped the enemy. Tinker prayed for the safety of his underbelly and cursed the Air Ministry for not issuing parachute bombs. He pulled his bomb-release toggle and a truck atomized. Some fascists tried to set up heavy machine guns on tripods, while others stood defiantly in the highway and shot at him with their rifles.

The Polikarpovs performed a wingover—a high, climbing turn and a dive wherein the biplanes resume their flight paths from the opposite direction—and again skimmed the ground. Tinker's run amounted to no more than 5 meters above the olive-green helmets and forage caps of the enemy. A cluster of Italians, who mounted an automatic weapon on the highway's shoulder, afforded him a tempting prize. Through his telescopic sight, Tinker traced his rounds as they inched toward the gun crew. A gentle push on the rudder pedals and the deadly geysers bowled over the anti-aircraft unit. Two soldiers, hunched beside the weapon, appeared to be taking a siesta. The Breda, manned by corpses, bucked wildly about on its stand, spewing death everywhere. At the apex of his wingover, beyond the impotent volleys sent skyward by the Italians, Tinker looked over at Gomez. The Guatemalan raised his clenched fist. "Salud!"

The dead were the lucky ones on the Saragossa-Guadalajara-Madrid highway that day. Those alive either tried to run, sought refuge in the shallow roadside gullies, or feigned death in hopes that the Red aviators would pass them by. Tinker's four fuselage-mounted Shkas machine guns worked in soviet to topple another gun crew whose members sought his life. Other soldiers fled as his fire dogged them close behind. The fascists flipped in midair and then came apart, their bodies offering the aspect of broken toy soldiers. The remaining Russian fighters performed oblique dives in every direction, blasting all fleeing Italians to be seen. Chatos and Moscas nearly collided as their masters feasted on the doomed enemy; wing-to-wing, the Polikarpovs dived, strafed, and zoomed upwards over the scene of carnage.

Tinker could see the dispirited troops cast down their rifles and run. The Italians seemed to have an aversion to dying alone as they bunched together in flight. At 700 feet, the enemy reminded Tinker of a swarm of ants running this way and that without a sense of direction. A slight adjustment to his

Chato's nose and the Arkansan activated his guns:

I could see dead-white faces swivel around and, at sight of the plane, terror would turn them even whiter. Some of them tried to run at right angles, but it was too late; already they were falling like grain before a reaper. I pushed the rudder back and forth gently, so that the bullets would cover a wider area, then pulled back on the stick just as gently; thus lengthening the swath. We kept this up until our gasoline and bullets were so low that we were forced to return to the field.

At the pilots' house that evening, the Americans learned that Loyalist troops had scotched the Rebel offensive that day and that wrecked Italian armor littered the Brihuega-Guadalajara highway for miles. Front-line communiques the following day, March 13, announced that Republican infantry had captured Trijueque and had severed the enemy's lines between Brihuega and Torija. Those Italians occupying Brihuega found themselves in danger of being overrun. General Roatta tried to bolster his front with Black Shirts and the Littorio Division, but these units were beaten back by the Loyalists. Clearing weather conditions allowed Nationalist aircraft over the battlefield, but the fascist planes too were driven back by swarms of Polikarpov fighters. Again and again, Republican air sorties hit the Rebels, including a strike by 28 groundstrafers against Italian columns on the Almadrones-Brihuega highway.

The exuberance manifested by this news was greatly tempered as a result of a tragedy that morning. During a bombing raid on truck convoys and designated freight trains between Jadraque and Sigüenza, the squadron came upon three fascist bombers. In the course of an ensuing attack by the I-15s, Lieutenant Antonio Blanch, the leader of LaCalle's third patrol, had his tail assembly shot away by one of the Savoia SM. 81 bombers from Tenento Colonnello Ferdinando Raffaelli's group, which was strafing the old Hispano-Suiza airfield. The Spaniard bailed out of his plane and pulled his parachute ripcord. To the horror of his squadronmates, Blanch's 'chute failed to open and the hapless aviator plummeted 6,500 feet to his death. By the time everyone had returned from the mission, Chang Selles met them at the airstrip with the flyer's mangled corpse. Somehow the horrible circumstances surrounding Blanch's death, coupled with the knowledge of Madrid's dependency on foreign aircraft and the occasional unevenness of its equipment and mechanics, gave Tinker a fleeting pang of mortality.

Tinker abandoned his gloomy ruminations on the morning of March 14 when LaCalle's squadron embarked on another bombing mission. No sooner had the American Patrol crossed into Rebel territory than it encountered a swarm of Fiats. La Calle waggled his wings as the danger signal and dropped his bombs. The remainder of the squadron followed suit and closed on their leader. The Fiats were to the left and higher than the Chatos, so LaCalle put the squadron in right echelon and began climbing and closing on the enemy. Their point formation, a seven-plane echelon, immediately engaged LaCalle's and Dahl's patrols. A second patrol of Fiats entered the fray as Tinker's unit arrived. For the Arkansan, that first rush of adrenaline heralded the beginning of the dogfight as he moved to activate his guns. With so many fighters in a confined space and traveling so fast, Tinker considered the awful possibility of being rammed. He cursed his luck as Fiat after Fiat zipped before his telescopic gunsight, affording him little more than tantalizing but ineffectual side shots.

TINKER'S FIRST KILL

Suddenly, however, Tinker drew behind a mottled green-and- beige Fiat and gave it a fifteen-second burst from his guns. When he disengaged, he noticed that his opponent was already in a spin earthward trailing gasoline, water, and greasy black smoke. The exhilaration of this sight captured his complete attention for a near-fatal moment-too-long. High above Tinker a Rebel patrol witnessed the American's first "kill," and now its leader and his cohorts came down on this Red pilot in search of revenge.

As the Fiat's tracers sped past his Polikarpov, Tinker could feel the 12.7 mm Breda rounds tear through his Chato—and he knew what was coming his way. Despite his contempt for Italian combat pilots, he had great respect for the contents of the Fiat's cartridge rotation: (1) TAT! an incendiary shell; (2) TAT! a soft-nosed nickel cartridge expanding bullet; (3) TAT! an explosive shell; (4) TAT! and finally, an ordinary 12.7 mm round capable of obliterating both man and machine. TAT-TAT-TAT-TAT! Over and over this lethal carousel played in Tinker's ears as he strove to escape.

Monitoring the lead Fiat's proximity to his tail in his rearview mirror, Tinker abruptly put his I-15 into a sharp left vertical bank. The CR 32 kept on in its original flight path carried by the fighter's forward momentum. Meanwhile, Tinker executed a 360-degree turn and came out directly behind his pursuer. He fired steadily at the fascist until the next Fiat lined up on him, and he performed the same maneuver on him, with the same results. This occurred twice more before he managed to conceal himself in a cloud bank.

Back at the aerodrome, news arrived that the Italians were in retreat all along the front and were suffering heavily from Republican air attacks.

Captured Italians substantiated these reports. These ragtag conscripts reported that they had not eaten in days because of logistical problems caused by the heavy rains; moreover, the enlisted men complained about the quality of leadership in their outfits, concluding that the division commander and two battalion leaders had been killed. Thoroughly confused, the common soldiers thought that they had been fighting in Ethiopia and were completely bewildered when many of them were taken prisoner by the Garibaldi Battalion, composed of Italian volunteers fighting for the Loyalist government.

Orders came on March 15 to escort 24 Breguet bombers to their targets. These crates were so slow that Tinker's Chato nearly stalled at 73 miles per hour. Despite this irksome handicap, however, the Breguets displayed unerring accuracy over the Italian positions destroying a mile and a half of trenches. As soon as the bombers departed, the accompanying I-15s began the usual fighter bombing and strafing routine. Over the rim of his cockpit, Tinker could see Republican tanks driving retreating Italian infantry before them in great haste. The fascists fled the battlefield down three roads, which converged at a crossroad. Their objective seemed to be a fourth highway which meandered from this juncture northward. At a critical moment when the traffic jam was at its worst, six Loyalist bombers appeared above and plastered the intersection. The slaughter was horrific, with huge troop transports blown high in the air and men flying from their open rear ends. As soon as the smoke cleared, Tinker's squadron and others went down to machine gun the survivors. Government tanks and cavalry closed the engagement, capturing sizable numbers of Italians, trucks, and field pieces. That afternoon LaCalle led another raid in support of Loyalist troops that were investing Brihuega. Circling high above the town, La Patrulla Americana provided protection for waves of Katiuska and Rasante bombers which blasted the suburbs of the town. When time permitted, the Chatos swooped down on enemy positions to complete the devastation. By nightfall, Brihuega once again belonged to the Republic.

Flying in squadrons of 15 planes, Gene Finick's Rasante groundstrafers attacked enemy infantry and armor repeatedly. The carnage wrought by Loyalist aircraft both fascinated and repulsed the American:

> Nothing that Hollywood ever turned out in mob scenes could touch it [Guadalajara] for action and horror. . . . Before that day's attack was done there must have been thirty thousand Italians scattered in mad flight all over the countryside. When nightfall came and we turned back from our last flight, they were still running for cover, and long lines of empty trucks and heavily loaded ammunition trains stood deserted on the highway that was supposed to take them to Madrid.

KOCH BOWS OUT

Charlie Koch's Russian Chato squadron also fought at Guadalajara. His outfit hit the Italian troops during sorties amounting to four or more daily. Toward the end of the week-long rout, Koch hemorrhaged after a raid and the medics rushed him to a field hospital. Ordered to Valencia, the physicians treated him for stomach ulcers and released him on condition that he return to America. Tiny Koch signed his severance papers from the Republican Air Force on April 8, 1937.

On March 17 LaCalle reorganized the squadron. Instead of the customary three patrols, as before, there were going to be four. He was to lead the first one, Dahl the second, Tinker the third, and Manuel Gomez the fourth. This new team met its test that afternoon when, while escorting a squadron of Rasante bombers over enemy territory, the patrols happened across three German Ju 52s ferried by twenty Fiats. LaCalle's pilots jettisoned their bombs and went into action.

TINKER'S SECOND VICTORY

LaCalle made a beeline for the Junkers; Dahl took on the Fiats to the left; Tinker offered combat to the CR 32s on the right, while Gomez climbed to meet the enemy flying high cover. The bombers unloaded their explosives and sped for home. Whitey's bold charge frightened the Fiats in his sector into the clouds. As Tinker passed through a cloud bank, he lost Justo García so that when he emerged on the other side, he had only one wingman, Rafael Magriña, still flying with him. Almost immediately they confronted three Fiats and closed on them in anticipation of a dogfight. Two of the fascist pilots fled, but one tried to outmaneuver his adversaries—with no luck at all. Tinker slipped behind the CR 32 and gave it continuous bursts for thirty seconds. The riddled Fiat went into a spin and hit the ground some 4,800 feet below. Meanwhile, Gomez had led his men against the patrol of Fiats overhead. At the point of engagement, he noticed with alarm that his wingmen had disappeared. The fascists made short work of a single Government fighter; so when the squadron returned to base, Gomez was missing. Despite a gloomy afternoon, everyone brightened that evening when LaCalle announced that their missing comrade had landed inside Loyalist lines, badly wounded.

On March 18, three air strikes began at 1:30 p.m., which consisted of both high altitude and low-level bombers together with strafing fighters. Half an hour later, two Republican divisions backed by 70 Soviet tanks attacked near Brihuega attempting to isolate trapped CTV troops. By 8:00 p.m., these Italian proxies were spared total annihilation with Rome's permission to retreat.

March 20 brought massive air sorties lasting for hours against evacuating Italian soldiers at Almadrones, Algora, and Navalpotro; despite attempts at intervention by Insurgent fighters, it seemed that no power on earth could stem the avenging tide of R-Zs, SB-2s, Chatos, and Moscas. Only the return of inclement weather precluded the complete destruction of Mussolini's volunteers from above.

Tinker would never forget his pride and exhilaration in a job well done that day.

> The trip back along the highway was quite interesting. The clouds were only about 1600 feet off the ground, so we were forced to fly very low. I was flying at an altitude of about 300 feet. . . . I would see a stream of their tracer bullets off on one side or the other and immediately dodge away from it, occasionally even dodging over or under the stream, which looked just like a stream of water from a hose. . . . Our troops immediately recognized the brilliant red markings on our planes and gave us a tremendous hand as we sailed by about ten feet off the ground. It gave them a big kick to see their own planes apparently ignoring the Italian antiaircraft as being too erratic to even bother about. They didn't know that the clouds forced us to fly so low. We could see them jumping up and down and giving us the Government military salute (clenched fist), which we returned.

During the Guadalajara offensive, not one Spanish Nationalist aircraft participated. The Legionary Air Force used every available plane, comprising Raffaelli's Savoia SM 81 group, Collacicchi-Sforza's Romeo Ro 37 group, and Fagnani's group of Fiat fighters, which were based at aerodromes in the province of Soria. The Loyalist Air Force employed a minimum of three Chato squadrons (LaCalle's and the Soviet units led by "José" [Ivan Kopets] and Kosokov) as well as the Mosca squadrons from Alcalá de Henares and the Rasante, Natacha, and Katiuska bomber groups. Conservative figures from Guadalajara put Italian losses at 500 killed, 2,000 wounded, and 500 prisoners of war plus massive stores of equipment. The battle of Guadalajara saved Madrid and with its salvation Tinker returned to his dogfights with the enemy.

PASSING THE TIME

The last third of March and the first few days of April brought continuous rain and precious few patrols. Card games and yarn-spinning passed the time, but the men of LaCalle's outfit wanted action. Personal involvement in multiple daily missions, the anticipation of the dogfight on any particular sortie, the thrill of the "kill," and the dread of being shot down, all of these emotions converged to boost the adrenaline level of these combat pilots. The members of Escuadrilla de Chatos had become addicted to the feel of the cockpit and the familiar whiff of oil, petrol, and metal. What constituted normal states of repose for most humans became unendurable for them, and they bridled at the very thought of hanging around the base for protracted stays.

Tinker liked to devise aerial maneuvers he would never employ in battle and generally good-naturedly ride herd on his mechanics. While on alert, he and the boys would sit on the dry, sandy ground close to their planes and play Julepe, gambling away their pay in this Spanish card game. The Spanish pilots were under the impression that Tinker and Dahl drew the pay of a second lieutenant–around 1,500 pesetas a month–instead of 18,000 pesetas as "contract men." For this reason Tinker preferred to keep the pot as low as possible. Both sides were great believers in *mañana*, and frequently they would progress so far toward a patrol as to warm up the engines and then cancel the mission, the excuse being given as "Mañana." During one particularly slow afternoon, an unwitting American aviator suggested that the squadron trench strafe the fascists during siesta. His commander became furious and warned the mercenary never to broach the issue again, reminding him that the enemy could do the same to them.

Tinker introduced the old Arkansas game of coin-pitching, the only modification being the use of the Spanish 5 peseta piece instead of a silver dollar. He and the other pilots would scoop out holes in the ground slightly larger than the coins about 20 feet apart. Then, one by one, the players assumed positions at one hole and tossed their coins at the other. The scoring followed the rules of horseshoe pitching: a coin in the hole counted for 5 points, otherwise the tosser closest to the hole got 1 point. The first participant to accrue 21 points, Tinker reminded his tarmac loafers, won the game and the loser's coin. When all other diversions failed, Tinker and associates staged centipede fights conducted in glass jars: "They were about four inches long, with powerful jaws, and seemed to be a trifle poisonous. They were also very hard to kill; the winner in one of their fights always bit off the head of the loser. . . . These fights would last for at least half an hour and whenever one ended . . . quite a few pesetas changed hands". Two extraordinary dogs provided companionship to the men. The first mongrel was the only shell-shocked canine Tinker had ever seen, and the animal possessed no attention span whatsoever. The other dog, a fine German Shepherd named Tarzan, always gave first warning when enemy bombers came overhead. Whenever Tarzan barked, everyone headed for shelter. What's more, Tarzan was able to distinguish between the sounds of Republican and Rebel bomber engines.

Base life for the Nationalist and Republican airmen was similar in military routine and leisure pursuits, as ideology bowed to the native pilots' commonality of culture and national experience. If the Rebel pilots enjoyed an edge, both on the ground and in the air, it was in the person of García Morato. Short and on the stocky side, he was an idol to his men, commanding their respect and friendship. The junior pilots and ground crewmen found him to be likable, unpretentious, and an incorrigible tease. Most of his senior pilots appreciated his unruffled manner and quiet demeanor, and were always careful never to presume upon his good nature. A few of those closest to him, however, resented his penchant for elevating flyers according to aerial competence rather than seniority. Even this circle, nevertheless, knew him to be the best damn combat pilot in Spain—bar none. Personal promotions and acclaim seemingly meant little to him, as he always had his fighter in readiness near his headquarters and flew regularly with his Fiat groups. Morato either joined the units on the way to the front or near the target area where he assumed command.

ESCUADRILLA DE LACALLE PASSES INTO HISTORY

Tinker thought it odd that during periods of great inactivity changes seemed to come in droves. Whitey obtained a medical furlough in Madrid due to stomach complications, and the brass transferred Selles to the Alcalá airstrip. Orrin Bell was unable to pass his flight checks and made his way back to the United States. Derek Dickinson failed as a combat flyer, but checked out as an observation pilot and was assigned to Barcelona. As mentioned, Allison and Koch were ordered back home because of medical problems. Finally, LaCalle's promotion to major and his reassignment abruptly ended the short, but illustrious history of Escuadrilla de LaCalle.

LaCalle considered Tinker the most qualified pilot to follow him as commander of the escuadrilla. The American had demonstrated excellent behavior over the front, a good combat record, and a remarkable sense of responsibility. Despite all of these positive attributes, Tinker spoke very poor Spanish. For this reason alone, LaCalle felt an obligation to choose Alonso Jiménez Bruguet. The Air Ministry had assigned La Calle (with eleven victories) to the Soviet Union as an instructor, together with the second contingent of aviators dispatched there for training. LaCalle would return to Spain during the battle of Teruel, but for a year he would serve as aide to the undersecretary for Air. During the closing months of the conflict, LaCalle rose to the rank of chief of staff of the Republican Fighter Squadron, of which he took command, and on November 30, 1938 he would be promoted to the rank of major.

WHITEY'S CONTINUING TRIBULATIONS

During this period Whitey Dahl's health was at risk in several ways. When his condition worsened at a Madrid hospital, he obtained a medical furlough to Paris on April 12 for an appendectomy, there to be joined by his wife. Since Dahl merited only a week's sick leave, the Air Ministry canceled his contract. When he ultimately returned to Spain on June 24 to collect his back pay, Ministry officials balked and even threatened to have him shot. Doubtless Whitey would have been executed had Spanish officialdom and its Russian allies known that this troublesome mercenary had given the U.S. military attaché in Paris full details with photographs of the Soviet I-15 pursuit before leaving France.

Following much deliberation, Dahl persuaded the Air Ministry of his good faith and with LaCalle's help he returned to combat. LaCalle would describe Whitey as being "even more aggressive than Tinker, but . . . he inspired less confidence in assuming the responsibilities as head of a squadron. He was a very good pilot without a doubt." As the Republic's ace of aces, a grateful LaCalle awarded Whitey five confirmed victories in Spain. Returning to combat, Dahl asked to be transferred to Commander Ivan A. Lakeev's Mosca squadron where Baumler and Tinker were then attached. Far less impressed with the American's sense of duty, especially in the company of Tinker and Baumler, the Air Ministry sent him to the Chato outfit.

On April 15, Tinker's squadron decamped for Teruel, the city that would cost more lives than any other in the Spanish war. Two days later, while napping under the wing of his fighter, he awakened to find his group in an emergency scramble. Tinker and his wingmen were aloft and reaching for altitude within seconds, allowing time for the entire escuadrilla to clear the runway. By now, the Arkansan commanded the unit as LaCalle's replacement; Alonso Jiménez had failed to meet the group's expectations. As a sop to air force authorities, the Spaniard remained in authority on the ground.

THE APRIL 17 AIR BATTLE

Tinker's new brood arrived over Teruel at an altitude of about 13,000 feet. At the far fringe of the city, the flyers spotted a crippled Katiuska bomber barely under way and in desperate need of escort protection. No sooner had all four patrols formed on the SB-2's tail than German fighters appeared, off to the right, and in three echelons of seven planes each. The enemy's lowest echelon was about 10,000 feet up, while its highest formation was on a plane with Tinker's squadron. The third fascist echelon had assumed an equidistant station at 11,500 feet, below the Chato formation. From the corner of his eye, Tinker glimpsed a patrol of I-16s closing on the lowest echelon of Heinkels and raising his eyes he saw a second swarm of Moscas ready to attack the intermediate group of He 51s from the rear. By this time, the ailing Katiuska had crossed safely into Government territory. Relieved of his charge, Tinker charged his guns and gave each of the four 7.62 mm Shkas a quick burst to warm the oil before assaulting the uppermost formation of Heinkels. With the morning sun at his back, Tinker hit the enemy hard.

With respect to this April 17 air battle, according to Angel Salas, three Spanish Nationalist squadrons were in operation with a total of 17 fighters. The 2nd squadron, comprised of five pursuits, caught sight of a Red bomber, but its machines were unable to close the distance. Soon thereafter, the squadron was joined by another Heinkel, flown by Second Lieutenant Jaime Palmero, and together these fascist pilots sighted Tinker's Chatos above them at 13,000 feet. The Heinkels climbed to engage, resolving to break formation at the instant of interception; a single I-15 flown by the Loyalist aviator Calvo, however, dived to meet the upcoming He 51s and collided with Palmero. The subsequent dogfight raged across the sky, with ten more Chatos and a third Republican pursuit unit joining the battle against the remaining planes of Salas' 2-E-2 Heinkel group. Bereft of the assistance of 2-E-2's two additional squadrons, off on patrol and ignorant of 2nd squadron's dilemma, the five Nationalist pilots engaged alone.

Salas performed attack passes on four enemy aircraft, dogfought, and landed at Calamocha with empty tanks; his mechanic counted eighteen bullet holes through his fuselage and wings. Three of his men trailed him to Calamocha with great damage to their Heinkels. The fifth pilot, Javier Allende, made a forced landing inside his own lines, near the front, having been downed by the Government ace Juan Comas Borrás. Both Palmero and the Republican pilot Calvo died in the early midair crash. On the evening of April 17, Salas received a congratulatory telegram from García Morato.

TINKER'S THIRD VICTIM

How different this contest appeared to Second Lieutenant Tinker! For a few seconds, the air seemed alive with dueling aircraft a mile and a half south of Teruel. Then two Heinkels wavered unsteadily out of the ball of men and machines, shuddered, and went into their final spins, which ended when they finally crashed to earth several miles below. A Mosca likewise emerged from the melee and collided with a Heinkel in a blinding flash. Nothing remained of the planes and their occupants save fragments of wings and tail assemblies drifting down slowly, cartwheeling as pieces of cardboard thrown into the wind from a high window.

Tinker's perception of the dogfight became rote as the aircraft of friend and foe alike slid across his gunsight. He reminded himself constantly not to fire on a comrade in the confusion and not to bank too sharply lest he lose consciousness and crash. Somehow oblivious to the possibility of his own death in this action, Tinker's recollection of his third victory seems almost clinical in retrospect:

> I see a green plane turning in toward me and I automatically pull over to meet him. I get there first—in line, that is—and open fire; steadily, this time. Although he never succeeds in getting in line I see his machine guns winking away and his tracers dripping blobs of smoke—as I suppose he sees mine—but he is just a trifle too late. First, metal starts flying from the left side of his motor, followed by water and black smoke. Then a line of fabric tatters works down the sleek side of the plane. As he goes past, his plane is in a sort of a sliding roll and is already headed for the ground, leaving a long thin trail of the unmistakable greasy black smoke. No need to bother about him any more.

Tinker and his comrades had switched formation on signal, jockeying for the best position from which to open the dogfight. This aerial foreplay preceded a solid wall of fire from the Polikarpovs. Dripping threads of gray smoke issued from the pointed noses of the Heinkels as they replied—tracers. One of the He 51s veered crazily, turning cartwheels as a child's kite gone awry. At this impromptu signal, the enemy group scattered. The contest rippled in an ever increasing arc, and the sky became crisscrossed by white vapor trails—a sight Tinker appreciated. At first his vision and reflexes sharpened; and as the whirling craft began to engage, he lost his sense of time and space. The Republican pilots locked on to their respective adversaries; Tinker framed a Heinkel in his sight. The Spaniard saw Tinker just as he fired a burst; he zoomed upward. Through his telescopic gunsight, he watched his rounds track over the fascist's head. The Arkansan eased the Chato's rudder, then lowered its snout somewhat. A red streamer flying from the Rebel's helmet caught his eye—the squadron commander.

Unbeknownst to Tinker, he had locked horns with Salas. Too intent on his prey, Tinker's plane rocked from the impact of unfriendly fire. As the He 51 flashed by close beneath him, he executed a tight wingover. The Heinkel banked to the right, so Tinker anticipated his making a right turn. He realized that his maneuverable I-15 could out turn his opponent. In the midst of the duel, another Heinkel flashed across Tinker's path and was awarded a hot broadside; it disappeared with another Chato in pursuit. Tinker kept to his opponent's tail. The He 51 went into an Immelmann—a half loop, the plane rolling right side up at the top—and before Tinker reacted, the Heinkel perforated his tail assembly. Tinker partially sideslipped the fusillade. Perhaps conceding greater experience and tactical awareness to Salas, but conscious of his own plane's superior power, armament, and agility, he never doubted the outcome. The Heinkel aped Tinker's sideslip, whereupon he whipped his Chato into a tight vertical turn. Still hounded by Salas, he rolled into a reversement, snapped out of a right vertical, and proceeded into one to the left. Cold fear followed anger as, for an instant, Tinker believed himself towing his enemy on an invisible rope. He began to loop, climbing away; then he stalled his ship near the top and both pilots passed as Tinker dived: a corkscrewing Chandelle, a tight climbing turn, as he eyed his pursuer over his shoulder. For a time, the two chased one another in a circle. At 240 miles per hour, the centrifugal force began to distort Tinker's mental processes. It became clear that someone had to break off the chase—and soon. Tinker knew that whoever bolted from the circle first would be momentarily exposed. A slight application of top rudder, and the Chato rocketed out of the ring. From his new perspective, Tinker seemed to be flying on his side along a horizon of clouds; he then found himself upside down, but his pull-up cost him momentum. Salas, just coming to his senses, flew directly opposite him. Tinker dropped back, swung behind, and fired.

His rounds stitched a staggered path of bullet holes along the bottom of the Heinkel's cockpit. The Saint Andrews Cross on the enemy plane's rudder seemed to disappear in a cloud of flying tracer, metal, and fabric. The Heinkel eluded his view. Tinker righted himself and prepared for another attack when he sighted the commander's plane again. Without warning, the enemy fighter slipped steeply; then it started to spin in the opposite direction, its motor wide open. The Heinkel vanished in a cloud. A momentary surge of exultation fell into uncertainty. What of the Spaniard? Far below, Tinker spotted a solitary enemy fighter skimming the ground in mad pursuit of his fellow airmen. His eyes focused on the mocking red streamer that fluttered from the pilot's helmet. It would take an angled dive and a quick burst to finish off the Insurgent, but Tinker had other fish to fry that afternoon.

Tinker's attention to his next intended victim was so intense that he failed to notice the Heinkel on his tail. Finally aware of his involvement in this daisy-chain of death, he executed a violent vertical bank to the left and watched as the Spaniard behind him continued on down in his dive. As he surveyed the sky, Tinker noted that the enemy had begun to break off the battle and dive clear of the Polikarpovs. All escaped save two He 51s, which had been cornered by Russian pilots in a small valley below; the demise of these careless fascists provided the Red Wings with entertainment as they began to regroup. Battle reports that evening put Spanish Nationalist losses at eight Heinkels to one Loyalist fighter—the Chato that collided at the outset of the fray.

Enough remained of the two collided planes and pilots for Loyalist medical examiners to deduce that the Government pilot had been hit in the neck, his jugular vein having been severed. It appeared to Tinker that the 7.92 mm bullet through Calvo's neck had momentarily dazed the mortally wounded flyer. Then Calvo regained consciousness and realizing that his end was near—unable to reach the ground in time to prevent a complete loss of blood—he deliberately gained altitude and rammed Palmero's Heinkel before passing out altogether. The young Spaniard's sacrifice had a profound effect on Tinker, who later characterized it as an "heroic gesture."

A new replacement returned with his plane riddled with bullets, but not a scratch on the pilot. The Soviet airman informed his mechanic that he had smelled the odor of burned wood while in the air; when the ground crewman examined the aviator's Mosca, he discovered that an incendiary shell had passed through both sides of the cockpit. A string pulled taut through both holes revealed that the round must have passed just under the Russian flyer's nose and was probably what he had smelled burning. Despite his ordeal, the Red pilot received a verbal reprimand and temporary grounding from his squadron commander. His superior officer reasoned that since most of the damage to the plane had been inflicted from the rear, obviously its occupant had spent the greater part of his air time fleeing the enemy.

Celebrating their perceived good fortune that evening at a nearby tavern, Tinker's people learned that they had bested "inexperienced" Spanish pilots earlier in the afternoon. Government intelligence disclosed that the fascist squadron commander had been flying for "only four months" and that his airmen possessed "no combat experience" at all. It seemed incomprehensible to Tinker that the "green" Spanish pilots could have been sent against LaCalle's seasoned veterans. For the better portion of the evening, he pondered this question as he consumed Sarrion's champagne stock and started on the local wines. Dawn brought Tinker an awful hangover.

It was true that Salas' 2nd squadron of Heinkel group 2-E-2 did not bear a distinguished record at this point in the war: its five members having accounted for six Republican aircraft; however, these combat pilots were good, and by war's end their combined record would swell to 32.5 victories.

On April 22 the first new Chato replacement fighter was sent to Tinker's squadron. Unfortunately an inexperienced Spanish pilot had been hurriedly assigned to the job of ferrying it to the airfield from the assembly plant in Los Alcázares. The novice tried three times to land downwind and crashed into Magriñá's I-15, which was parked a hundred yards from Tinker's machine. The Spaniard emerged unscathed while destroying both aircraft. Tinker's hot-blooded wingman drew his pistol to kill the flyer, but was stopped in time by a colleague. Magriñá's Russian allies, however, made life very hard on the boy aviator.

HEMINGWAY AND THE HOTEL FLORIDA

The American Patrol's tour of duty on the Teruel front ended on April 24, 1937, with orders to return to the old airfield at Campo X. Major LaCalle paid his former understudies a surprise visit the following day; when he saw the weary faces of Tinker and three of the original twelve pilots from his old squadron, he awarded the survivors a week's leave. Without a moment's hesitation, Tinker and two Spanish compatriots departed for Madrid and the Hotel Florida. He subsequently recalled:

> I lost no time in locating the Americans who were staying there. They were mostly writers and newspaper people—[Herbert] Matthews, of the *New York Times*; Martha Gellborn and Ernest Hemingway; [Henry] Gorrell, of the United Press. There were also a few members of the Abraham Lincoln Brigade there. All had jammed themselves into Hemingway's room on the second floor. Hemingway was to leave

for Paris the following day. They were throwing a farewell party in his honor.

The conversation was just getting lively when I heard a shrill whistling sound, followed by a loud explosion and a lot of clattering. I jumped up and went to the window. A shell had struck the decorative top of the Paramount Theater just across the Plaza de Callao. I looked at the others. Oh, that's the beginning of the usual afternoon bombardment, said one. The conversation continued, as lively as before. The only one who paid any attention to the explosives was a young photographer who dashed out to get pictures.

The friendship of Tinker and Hemingway held together through mutual respect. The American flyer admired the celebrated journalist's genius as a writer, the reports of his courage in the face of dangerous front-line situations, his public displays of gregariousness and ebullience of spirit, and his seeming lack of pretense and sanctimoniousness. Most of all, Tinker was touched by his friend's almost childlike faith in the Republican cause. For his part, Hemingway appreciated the mercenary as a drinking partner and boon companion, his high degree of intelligence, his unique way of crafting southern idioms, and his usually restrained demeanor which seemed to reassure and calm his men at critical moments. What seized Hemingway's imagination, however, was the young man's membership in a technological priesthood, a man among men who could practice society's oldest art form, killing, with the touch of a button and the pull of a lever. Well plied with amber cheer at a Madrid or Valencia watering hole, Hemingway was known to become emotional and blurt out to passing flyers words to the effect: "this is a land of peasants. You are professionals, you know machines and how to make them work. We don't. You know how to fight machines, so help us."

Porters and patrons alike at Madrid's Hotel Florida frequently witnessed Tinker's crew of airmen in drinking bouts, gambling marathons, and bull sessions with Hemingway, Herbert Matthews, Martha Gellhorn, and officers and men of the Lincoln Brigade on leave from the front. These airmen and brigaders were ubiquitous, milling in and out of Papa's hotel suite, swapping war news and personal gossip, availing themselves of their host's tub, consuming spirits and edibles found there, and making a good faith effort not to disturb him as he typed dispatches for the North American Newspaper Alliance. Although Tinker would have flown and fought for his found at this point in the war, still it took him aback to discover that these idealistic foot-sloggers made only 10 pesetas a day. "Hell, that was no money at all," he muttered. Some of the Lincolns disliked the well-paid "volunteer" aviators, and even resented their host for his special status as a noncombatant. As Hemingway saw it, they had volunteered, both he and the mercenaries had contracted for a job. What were they grousing about? A dyed-in-the-wool Southerner, Tinker was baffled by the title "Lincoln" Battalion. "Why not a Jeff Davis Battalion?" he once inquired.

In his short story, *Night Before Battle*, Hemingway chronicled an evening with the U.S. flyers from Alcalá de Henares. Having paid Hemingway a brief visit, Tinker returned to the aerodrome. His companions showed up and, having just missed their squadronmate, decided to stay for a bath and the opportunity to establish a crap game. To a man, the flyers remained with the dice on the sitting room floor, quarreling among themselves, inviting others to join their circle of chance, but never dispersing to mix with Papa's other guests. The brigaders stayed clear of the game, intimidated by the worldly, high-rolling, contract warriors who earned $1,500 each month. Hemingway's friend and IB tank corpsman Al Wagner eventually lost his shirt to these knights of the air.

In subsequent passages, Hemingway and his fictional brigader friend encounter one of the American pilots on the elevator. Sequentially referred to as "the wooly jacket man" and "a rummy fake Santa Claus," the intoxicated Baldy Jackson was Hemingway's fictional surrogate for Harold Evans (Whitey) Dahl. Bad-natured banter developed between airman and tanker, and Jackson (Dahl) threatened Wagner with a champagne magnum over his head. When tempers cooled, the reeling pilot explained the reason for his drunkenness before everyone in Hemingway's room, including Jackson's fellow aviators, now standing erect.

The conversation turned to the February 18 aerial battle in which Jackson (Dahl) lost his Chato fighter. The band of airmen wanted to attribute Baldy's (Dahl's) bad luck to a panicky wingman who reputedly fled before the attacking Fiats, but Jackson only blamed himself. In dramatic fashion, the stocky flyer with a cherub's florid visage slurred through his rendition of how he had flamed a Junkers bomber, became enraptured by the sight of the burning hulk, and exposed his I-15's stern to the guns of a diving Fiat.

Turning to Hemingway's comrade, Al Wagner, one of the flyers asked: "Is he in tanks?" "Yes. He's been there since the start." "They get ten pesetas a day," Henry (Hemingway) said. "Now he gets a lieutenant's pay." "Spanish lieutenant?" "Yes." "I guess he's nuts all right. Or has he got politics?" "He's got politics." "Oh, well," he said. "That explains it." Jackson (Dahl) continued his account of the February 18 dogfight:

> We were in a left echelon of Vs. Then we went into a left echelon of echelons and dove onto them with all four guns until you could have touched them before we rolled out of it. We crippled three others [bombers]. The Fiats were looming up in the sun. They didn't come down until I was sightseeing all by myself.

When I banked out of it I looked down and of course she [the Ju 52] had been pouring black smoke but she was holding right on her course to get over the mountains. She was losing altitude fast and I came up and over and dove on her again. There were still wingmen there, and she'd lurch and started to smoke twice as much and then the door of the cockpit came open and it was just like looking into a blast furnace and then they started to come out . . . then one [parachute] started to burn at the edge and as it burned the man started to drop fast and I was watching him when the bullets started to come by and the Fiats right behind them and the bullets and the Fiats.

"Come on, Baldy [Dahl]. You drunken sleepy bum." "Not me," said Baldy. "I am a potential ace of the people's army." "Takes ten [5] to be an ace. Even if you count Italians, you've only got one, Baldy." "It wasn't Italians," said Baldy. "It was Germans. And you didn't see her when she was all hot like that inside. She was a raging inferno."

"I'm sorry about the game [Henry/Hemingway]." "They'd have broke me anyway. Those guys are poisonous with dice. . . . They're strange guys, too. I guess they don't get overpaid. I guess if you are doing it for dough there isn't enough dough to pay for doing it [Wagner]."

Hemingway knew Tinker and Dahl to be extraordinary pilots: Tinker, the cool hunter who relied on his tactical genius, and Dahl, the aggressive, aerial killer whose head-on maneuvers placed himself and the enemy at equal risk. This strange man of immoderate habits and eccentric behavior flew and fought brilliantly, but his reckless style of combat made him vulnerable at every turn. Hemingway considered him the quintessential primitive among his peers, already an anachronism in the relatively short history of aerial warfare.

On the ground, however, Whitey's antics and self-deprecating humor amused Hemingway no end. Fifteen years after one particular conversation with Dahl concerning the flyer's larcenous proclivities, Hemingway shared its sidesplitting substance with American art critic and expatriate, Bernard Berenson:

I know only a little about stealing pictures, but the funniest one I know was a flyer named Whitey Dahl. He was a very good flyer and he came to me one day and said: "Mr. Ernest, I'd like you to give me an opinion." "Sure," I said. "Is Van Dick a good painter?" He pronounced it that way. "Very good painter, Whitey. Well thought of." "What would a good Van Dick be worth?" "I cannot tell you Whitey, exactly. I'd have to find out. But it would be worth a considerable sum of money." "Well, I'm certainly glad to hear that," Whitey said. "I'm glad to know my judgment is good. I picked up that old Van Dick when we were first out at the castle and I carry it with me everywhere and it hangs over my bed. I love that old Van Dick and I'm certainly glad to hear you confirm that I've got good taste."

Dahl solemnly promised Hemingway that he would surrender the art treasure after the war, but he was shot down and captured before his pledge could be fulfilled.

Those brigaders who filled Papa's apartment in the Hotel Florida were but a fraction of their comrades to be found in the streets of Madrid. What a dashing figure they cut in their ski pants, boots, and jaunty berets! These smart khaki-and-blue denim uniforms seemed to overpower the ragamuffin attire of the average citizen. Lincolns flooded the hotels, the Florida and the Nacional, and entranced the Madrileños there with their cockiness. Municipal bars such as Chicotes and the Aquarium suffered large delegations of these empty-pocketed volunteers, who believed that their individual sacrifices merited company and a drink. A loyal gang of soldiers always piled into the Capital cinema where dated Hollywood productions were shown to truly international audiences.

Tinker strolled past residences and apartment buildings with the dollhouse effect: a dwelling with a wall sliced away and exposing rooms with twisted beds, smashed sideboards, and suspended chandeliers hanging over an abyss, a dining room table with its setting in place while everything else had been obliterated. He stopped to watch the division El Campesino parading up the Calle de Alcalá with flags aflutter and shouldered Italian arms captured at Brihuega. The troops in buff appeared healthy, their faces rouged by the biting winds of the sierras.

The city remained under fire from German artillery secreted on Monte Garabitas, the highest elevation of the Casa de Campo on Madrid's western border. The fascists scheduled their bombardments to coincide with theater closings on the Gran Via in late afternoon. Huddled pedestrians scurried along for fear of being killed by exploding shells. The dry, whacking shocks of detonating rounds in the streets were followed by yellow smoke and the odor of granite dust that shrouded the environs of the impact center. Soldier and civilian alike enjoyed a ride to the trenches by streetcar, costing 10 centimos. At certain locations, Republican and Nationalist positions were not more than 50 meters apart. U.S. volunteers devoted much of their furloughs to the inspection of the capital's fortifications as Madrid represented an extension of Brunete.

By day, Tinker relished trips to the front lines where he took potshots at Rebel infantry; by night, he savored the social offerings of Madrid. While on such a nocturnal outing, an artillery shell destroyed his hotel room and ruined two bottles of Scotch whiskey hidden behind his bathtub. Irate, Tinker swore revenge.

I was so enraged by the incident that I was still rather fluently cursing the Fascists when I went below to see the management about getting another room. I even went so far as to forget that other people might be able to understand English, until I was reminded of this fact by Miss [Martha] Gellhorn, who happened to be sitting in the lobby at the time.

The shell in my room had one good result, though; the management moved me down to the second floor on the safe side of the building. . . . The following day Franco planted another shell right through the sidewalk in front of my favorite lobby window. . . . This shell failed to explode, which saved the life of the newspaper vendor who had his wares laid out on the window ledge. It went completely through the pavement and lodged about three feet under the surface . . . breaking three of the four big lobby windows, and giving the newsboy, who was standing about five feet from where it hit the side-walk, a choice collection of scratches and bruises. On this occasion I happened to be across the street in the Paramount Theater marveling at the fact that Popeye and Mickey Mouse could speak better Spanish than I could.

An attractive companion named Dolores filled his hours, despite the constant danger from repeated shelling. In a bar, in the streets, in a theater, they could not escape the whine of projectiles and the concussive force of nearby explosions. Under these conditions, Tinker welcomed the unexpected appearance of Major LaCalle at his hotel room, and he eagerly hitched a ride with him back to Campo X.

Once there, Tinker suffered Maria's bad temper, as she had heard of his carousing in various Madrid nightclubs with another female companion. Maria once lived in the capital, and she knew these places to be dens of iniquity. Tinker hastened to assure her that these haunts had become quite respectable since her departure from the city; as for Dolores, well, he was escorting her for a friend. At the first opportunity, Tinker persuaded his wingmen to back up his story and strengthened his case with bars of American and English toilet soap.

(Standing left to right) Tinker, a mechanic, Riverola, Gil, Casteneda, Captain LaCalle, Velasco; (Seated) Bastido, Whitey Dahl, Chang Selles, and Lecha. *Copyright 1938 by Funk & Wagnalls Company. Copyright renewed. Reprinted by permission of HarperCollins Publishers, Inc.*

Tinker and his Russian plane. *Copyright 1938 by Funk & Wagnalls Company. Copyright renewed. Reprinted by permission of HarperCollins Publishers, Inc.*

FEBRUARY 1937

Fecha	Piloto	Tipo y numero del avion	Pasajero	Tiempo	Lugar	Objeto del vuelo	Observaciones	Motor
2	Self	Masca #56	Nada	:50	At [illegible]	Squadron Practise	Fair formations	Wright Cyclone
3	"	"	"	1:05	"	Cross Country To Albacete	"	"
4	"	"	"	:05	Albacete	Formation Practice	Excellent formation	"
5	"	"	"	:50	"	Dog-fight with Russian Squadron	shot down [illegible]	"
6	"	"	"	:15	"	Takeoffs + Landings	None	"
7	"	"	"	1:45	" To Guadalajara	Cross-Country To Guadalajara		"
10	"	"	"	:45	"	(Bombardment Missions	Across lines.	"
10	"	"	"	:50	"	Squadron (11) dropped 90 Bombs	Also M.G. fire)	"
* 11	"	"	"	:40	"	" (lost mechanic) 40	" " " "	"
11	"	"	"	:25	"	To Field X	Nada	"
12	"	"	"	1:15	"	(Bombardment of Enemy	Concentration)	"
12	"	"	"	:50	"	(Its Much A.A. But No	damage)	"
13	"	"	"	:30	"	Bombardment + M.G.	(Kept out of Line	"
13	"	"	"	:20	"	Defense of Madrid	Returned to Field	"
14	"	"	"	x :20	To Campo X	X-Country	Excessive Vibration	"
15	"	"	"	:20	Madrid	2 Test-Hops — No change		"
16	"	"	"	:15	"	Test Hop - O.K.		"
16	"	"	"	:45	"	Defense of Madrid	Squadron downed "One Junkers"	"
17	"	"	"	:50	"	"	Chased 24 Fiats [illegible]	"
17	"	"	"	:15	"	Test-Hop	O.K.	"
† 18	"	"	"	1:05	"	Defense of Madrid	[illegible] Landed O.K.	"
18	"	"	"	1:00	"	"	Shot at 3 Junkers	"
19	"	"	"	:25	"	To Repel Invaders	Invaders Repelled	"
19	"	"	"	1:15	"	Defense of Madrid	Couldn't find Enemy	"
				17:25				

Brought Forward = 20:25

Total = ~~27:10~~ 37:50

* Calderon (by A.A.)

† Lando Killed in Crash Landing

NOTA: [illegible]

Twenty-four flights made in sixteen days—pages from Tinker's official flight log book. *Copyright 1938 by Funk & Wagnalls Company. Copyright renewed. Reprinted by permission of HarperCollins Publishers, Inc.*

Tinker (right) with Chang Selles, whose disappearance developed one of the war's strangest stories. *Courtesy Frank G. Tinker, Jr.*

(Standing) Three mechanics; (Seated left to right) Whitey Dahl, Chang Selles, and Tinker. A Polikarpov I–15 can be seen in the background. *Courtesy Frank G. Tinker, Jr.*

Tarzan, the bomber hound. His warnings of raids anticipated all others. *Courtesy Frank G. Tinker, Jr.*

Lieutenant Orrin Bell.

BEN LEIDER
AMERICAN HERO

**DIED
FIGHTING
FOR
DEMOCRACY**

●

**MADRID
FEB. 19
1937**

●

FIVE CENTS

Courtesy of the Newspaper Guild.

Why the Memorial?

WHEN the flash came over the wires telling us that our friend, Ben Leider, had been killed in Spain, those of us who knew and loved him felt that yielding to natural grief would be an insult to the memory of an American fighting man.

We knew, as surely as if he had told us, just what we were to do.

It was as if he had said: "I have done my share, go now and do yours."

Spontaneously then, we met, and with an amazing singleness of purpose we proceeded with the formation of the committee. Spontaneously, too, as soon as the word got out, money poured into the coffers and before the committee was a week old, it had distributed almost a thousand dollars among several organizations already sending money to Spain for food, clothing and medical services.

Freedom and Democracy—these were things Ben Leider loved above all things. And what better memorial to Ben than a fund for the battle for Democracy?

He gave his life for that cause, what will you give?

THE COMMITTEE
HEYWOOD BROUN
Chairman

545 Fifth Avenue Room 910 MU. 2-6544

I enclose $.. as my contribution to the Ben Leider Memorial Fund.

I volunteer my services to the work of the Fund.

I will sell .... pamphlets.

Name ....

Address ....

Telephone ....

Courtesy of The Newspaper Guild.

Charles D. Koch in his junior year at the University of Georgia (1916).

6

FLYING WITH THE RUSSIANS

He had never thought that today would be his last. What does an atheist think of at the End?

Was he heroically inspired, uplifted with political fervor as he drew his last breath? I do not believe so. The ugliness of Death at her approach must drive away the paltry dream. He died in a lovely country in the sunshine . . .

I am sorry that I ever thought badly of these Russians; they have certainly paid dearly on this trip.

Olof de Wet
The Cardboard Crucifix

CAMPOSOTO AERODROME

On May 3 a staff car arrived from Alcalá with news that the Spanish Air Ministry had transferred Tinker and A. J. (Ajax) Baumler, the only two American fighter pilots remaining in Spain, to a crack Russian squadron stationed at Camposoto Airfield. As Baumler chauffeured him to their new base that very afternoon, it struck Tinker as amusing that this move advanced him both militarily and socially, since he came from an airstrip situated on the estate of a former count to one located on the grounds of a former duke.

Camposoto aerodrome was completely hidden from the enemy as its camouflage defied detection from the air. Tinker found it to be so narrow that it could only be used from two directions, east and west. The airstrip had a false winding road traversing it and several counterfeit ditches to blend the installation into the countryside. Its southern boundary constituted an actual stream, and below this creek stood a grove of trees which concealed the buildings. There were several wide bridges across the tributary suitably camouflaged, and when fighter aircraft landed they taxied across the bridges and parked under the huge oak trees. Since Camposoto was the closest Republican airfield to Madrid, it proved to be indispensable.

Tinker and Ajax made their initial flights with the Russians on the morning of May 5, when the entire squadron demolished a railroad station and freight train at a small town called Espinoza de Henares. On the return leg of the mission, Tinker's engine stopped five times before he reached Camposoto. Despite the prestige associated with his membership in the Soviet group, Tinker had not "traded up" with respect to aircraft. Flying over Rebel territory in an aging fighter presented a clear and present danger to the Arkansan.

Five days later, Tinker and two other pilots were flying over the Madrid-Burgos highway. Happening on a Rebel convoy, the triad formed at the rear of the column for a strafing run. Uniformed soldiers fell from truck cabs either dead or in flight to escape the Red Wings. Rattled drivers crashed into the caravan's preceding vehicle or drove off the shoulder of the road and down the mountainside in vain attempts to escape. Looking over his shoulder, Tinker began humming "She'll be coming 'round the mountain" in synchronization with the wide-open roar of his engine. His Soviet associates repeated this terrible scene twice more before leaving the fascist corpses to the sun and the vultures.

LIFE AT CAMPOSOTO

At Camposoto airfield, situated on the estate of the duke of Albuquerque, Tinker and Baumler lived in the main house, sleeping in one of the former nursery rooms on the second floor. The Americans shared their room with two Spaniards who liked the room hermetically sealed at night. The bedroom had two French doors which opened onto a large terrace built above the front veranda of the house. Before retiring either Tinker or Baumler would open the doors for air during the night; the Spanish flyers, however, closed them soon thereafter. Unhappy with the stuffiness of their sleeping quarters, they pushed their beds out on the terrace, much to the chagrin of the native pilots and Russians who believed that night air could be lethal. The house staff moved tables and chairs outside and cleaned the terrace regularly. Squadron leader Kosokov pronounced these sleeping arrangements as ridiculous, despite the fact that the flight surgeon sided with Tinker. Frank took his revenge on the Soviets by releasing harmless water snakes into their rooms.

Russian airmen and mechanics generally accepted with grace the Americans' penchant for banter and pranks, drawing the line only when it came to politics. Tinker occasionally recalled with bemusement the two Reds who had been attached to the Escuadrilla de Chatos during the Jarama campaign. Elias, the squadron's Spanish-Russian interpreter and Mikael, LaCalle's chief armorer, prided themselves on their knowledge of world affairs. Elias once jokingly asked Tinker if the report was true that Huey Long was president of the United States. The Soviet linguist was assured that the Kingfish had been liquidated the preceding year, and a bit later Tinker asked his comrade, with a straight face, if it was true that Leon Trotsky was supreme ruler of the Soviet Union. His retort incensed the Russians and nearly provoked a brawl. In time Mikael forgave his ally, but Elias bore a grudge against Tinker for the remainder of his tour.

NEW AERIAL STEEDS

Complications with the new Russian Cyclone engines nixed earlier orders for Tinker and Baumler to transfer to Santander. Despite the Air Ministry's refurbishment of their old Chato fighters with new Soviet-built powerplants, Madrid did not want any foreign volunteer pilots falling into Nationalist hands as a result of unproven engines. Unable to relocate and unburdened with military action, the Americans spent their time swimming, strolling in the woods near Camposoto, attending dog and cock fights, and courting the señoritas.

The enjoyment of music was a favorite pastime at Camposoto. Tinker liked to accompany the drome's best guitarist and baritone singer, a huge Russian named Basilio, on the accordian. Since neither man knew the songs of the others' homeland, both entertainers settled on Spanish favorites. Whenever "La Paloma" and "Cielito Lindo" were offered, an approving audience would drown out the performers. The best concerts were given inside the base's bomb shelter during night raids. Tinker recalled: "The bomb shelter had certain resonant acoustical properties that gave our respective instruments tonal qualities which they were never able to achieve above ground—the sort of rolling resonance you get when you shout into an empty rain barrel or an abandoned well." At the conclusion of every mission the Americans also looked forward to playing the Italian opera *Rigoletto* on their prized victrola. Hearing this piece over and over seemed to calm their frayed nerves.

During this imposed vacation, several major incidents occurred. As full-fledged members of an all-Russian squadron, Tinker and Baumler were the first non-Soviet aviators to be awarded I-16s by their hosts. The Russians also informed their American allies that Chang Selles, one of the original members of the American Patrol, had been arrested and shot. It seemed that Alcalá authorities executed the colorful flyer for spying against Russian aviation units for the Japanese government. Tinker swallowed hard when he recalled that Selles had borrowed his fountain pen almost daily to draft letters to his "sister" in Tokyo, and he reminded the Soviets and LaCalle that he had been an innocent accessory to the fact. The American went to his grave in the mistaken belief that his friend had been shot for treason. Doubtless, Selles' ancestry became the subject of Soviet suspicion due to the deterioration of Soviet-Japanese relations as a result of Tokyo's adventurism in China, but Chang never faced a Loyalist firing squad.

All through May, Tinker and Baumler spent their time becoming accustomed to the I-16 Mosca. Both men insisted to their Russian allies that the pursuit was nothing more than an advanced version of the U.S. Army P-26. The principal developments, argued Tinker, were the retractable landing gear and the more powerful motors, Soviet Cyclones. The I-16's armament consisted of two machine guns mounted in the wings and a pair in the engine cowling. Each gun fired, outside and inside of the propeller radius, at the then unbelievable rate of 1,800 rounds per minute, giving a combined volume of 7,200 rounds per minute. It reassured Tinker to know that he could nearly disintegrate a Fiat or a Heinkel with the slightest motion. Less reassuring was the incredible agility of the stubby fighter. Every time Tinker forgot and tried to employ biplane tactics, the Mosca went into a right spin. The Americans learned the hard way that most of the controlling had to be done with ailerons and flippers; very little rudder was required, even in steep banks.

THE ENEMY PREPARES

While the American flyers vacationed at Camposoto, the enemy reorganized and grew stronger. The Spanish Nationalist Fiat group, with the designation 2-G-3, was formed in Cordoba on May 4, from the squadrons 1-E-3 and 2-E-3 led by Morato and Salas. Morato assumed the station of group commander and Julio Salvador took over leadership of his old squadron.

During the months of May and June, Group Commander Morato did not lose a single fighter and succeeded in destroying 26 Red machines. In terms of Nationalist and Republican air strength in this period, at the end of May, with the arrival of a third Italian convoy stored Fiats were assembled in Seville to form a second Italian group and a second Spanish Nationalist squadron. Now there were the 16th Fighter Group la Cucaracha and the 23rd Fighter Group As de Bastos. La Cucaracha operated in the north and As de Bastos in central Spain. During the early summer of 1937, there were thirteen Government fighter squadrons (six of Mosca, all Russian, and seven of Chato, of which three were Spanish) opposing eleven Nationalist fighter squadrons, ten of Fiats (including the two from the Morato Group) and one of BF 109Bs.

TINKER'S FOURTH

On June 1, Group 2-G-3 was transferred from Saragossa to Avila. Once stationed, the unit escorted Romeo Ro 37 light bombers in attacks near La Granja and participated in low-level strafing and dive-bombing. Due to a scarcity of pursuits, Morato ordered a standing patrol beginning June 2. These patrols, amounting to two Fiats at a time, immediately accounted for three Rasantes and a Mosca.

On June 2, two Fiat squadrons from the As de Bastos Italian group arrived in the north to fight against Tinker's unit. Meanwhile the Americans had been spending several days escorting Rasante bombers over the Sierra to harass the Nationalist trenches just outside the city of Segovia. In a confrontation with a Fiat on June 2, Tinker recorded his fourth victory. His first burst disabled the CR 32, and his second killed the Italian as he prepared to jump. He did not intend to murder the helpless fascist, but he could not stop his guns from firing: "So there was nothing to do about it but hope that it [the pilot] might have been one of Mussolini's relatives." On the last of four sorties that day, the squadron became involved in a huge dogfight. Approximately fifty assorted Fiats and Heinkels came against the Republican formations from out of the sun. Tinker noticed a Fiat on the tail of a Chato. He immediately kicked his Mosca into a right half roll and fell behind the overconfident enemy pilot. A single burst of machine gun fire set the Fiat's motor ablaze. As the fascist began his downward plunge, Tinker disengaged to protect the last of the Rasantes. Before he could reach the beleaguered bomber, however, its tormentors had ignited the machine's fuel tanks, and down it went. Pilot and gunner bailed out of the inferno and drifted down into enemy territory. The day's tally ran to nine Rebel planes destroyed to two Loyalist machines and the ill-fated Rasante.

FINICK'S ORDEAL

Gene Finick's Rasante squadron had flown five missions daily in the May 31 Republican push to capture Segovia on the Guadarrama front. The missions went well in the beginning, but on the third day enemy resistance stiffened. On that day, the 4 groundstrafers and 25 escort fighters challenged an artillery battery at La Revenga. Once over his target, Finick's Rasante came under attack by 50 Heinkels and Fiats. Explosive bullets sailed through his wings, and the aileron controls snapped off. When Finick lost air speed, the other groundstrafer/bombers abandoned him. Continued enemy attacks set his plane on fire, and the possibility of an explosion forced Finick and his gunner to bail out. Falling a 1,000 meters without his parachute opening, he tore the 'chute open with his bare hands—it finally deployed. In the process of drifting toward his own lines, a marauding Fiat attempted to strafe him. Finick began swinging his chords from side to side, offering the Italian flyer a moving target. At this perilous moment, a Mosca came to his rescue. At first, Finick caught in a tree, then fell to earth and broke his leg. No sooner had he extinguished a small fire on his person, than he came under a hail of bullets from Loyalist soldiers who mistook him for the enemy. Fortunately the squad's commanding officer saved his life, and he was taken to a field infirmary for treatment. Finick went from hospital to hospital and endured several operations; despite the fact that his right leg was one centimeter shorter, he learned that he could fly again. Ajax Baumler and Tinker visited him in the hospital, where he languished for months before returning to the United States.

CATALONIAN INTERLUDE

On June 11 the Mosca squadrons led by Ukov and Lakeev arrived at Barbastro in Catalonia. The I-16s were flown by Russians, with the noted exceptions of Tinker and Baumler. Concomitantly, Republican SB-2 and Rasante bombers were making repeated attacks on Saragossa in preparation for the offensive at Huesca. In the course of aerial combats that followed, the Morato group shot down five Government planes. On June 12, Tinker flew five sorties escorting bombers, but logged no mention of dogfights. That same day, Morato's 2-G-3 experienced two brushes with I-16 formations. On their second mission over Huesca the Spanish Nationalist pilots destroyed four Moscas. On another June 12 patrol over the Huesca front, which was flown by Morato, Salas, and Guerrero, four Russian tanks were strafed and bombed. From the air, Morato also spotted a staff car which he machine gunned as it vainly sought to escape. That evening, Radio Barcelona announced that the leader of the Loyalist forces in the sector, General Matazalka Kemeny Lukács, had been killed by a solitary enemy fighter. Hungarian-born General Lukács commanded the 12th International Brigade. He had participated in the defense of Madrid during the fall of 1936, and he led his troops at Guadalajara. Besides General Lukács, the Morato Group also bagged two Rasante bombers.

TINKER AND BAUMLER SCORE

On June 14, Tinker's squadron and two Chato escuadrillas dogfought with 60 Fiats and Heinkels, a combined number of more than 100 machines in the air. Morato's group claimed the destruction of six Red fighters. Tinker conceded the loss of three I-15s, but recorded 14 Insurgent planes down. Somewhere in this web of claims and counterclaims, Ajax Baumler shot down a Fiat. On June 16, the final air battle over Huesca, Tinker's Red Wings faced 50 Fiats and Heinkels and destroyed 5 enemy aircraft, forfeiting one Rasante. The Arkansan flamed a CR 32, making it his fifth victory. Two days later, the Republicans raided Huesca with several squadrons of Katiuskas and three of Rasantes, shepherded by five squadrons of Polikarpovs. With such a large aerial armada, the city was severely damaged.

After the bombers left, all that could be seen of Huesca was a huge cloud of black smoke slowly rising from the wreckage of the city. . . . After the bombers finished their work, the fighters began strafing the trenches around the city. . . . Ukov and I were coming up after one of these strafing dives when a burst of antiaircraft fire exploded about forty feet behind my plane. . . . Ukov had seen the flashes of guns, which were located in a church belfry. We were so close to them that it would have been rather dangerous to try dodging them as usual, so we banked around and went for them, with our guns hammering away for all they were worth. This manoeuver was a stroke of genius; the surprised gunners were in a hail of bullets before they even realised what was happening; they didn't have a chance. As soon as we flashed past the belfry we clutched for the ground and then went far enough back into our own territory to be out of range of other guns before climbing for altitude. (Tinker)

On June 19, bad news reached Barbastro that the Basque capital of Bilbao had been occupied by the Navarrese Brigades. With Bilbao lost, there no longer existed a need to continue the Huesca struggle, so Tinker's group of Moscas moved to Liria and Los Alcázares.

A WAR WOUND?

After Huesca, Tinker and several of his Red cronies merited a two-week furlough beginning on June 21 at Costa del Sol. Al Baumler wangled a special trip to Valencia, but Frank and the Russians dallied, so they had to settle for the accommodations of a country villa formerly owned by a wealthy Alicante businessman. Affectionately dubbed the "Russian Villa," the place was operated by a young physician and his wife. Life at this rest and relaxation center seemed all that one could ask, as described by a grateful American guest: "Our usual schedule was to get up around nine, eat breakfast, and then go for a swim. Lunch, and then a two or three hour siesta. After that we would read, write, play croquet or tennis. The evening meal was a banquet. All kinds of food, wines, liquors and brandies. However, all this was too good to last."

Tinker's idyllic respite lasted only until June 25. That evening, the American, left alone at the villa, became uproariously drunk and embarked for Valencia on a bicycle—a distance of some 150 miles. By midnight he found himself 15 miles up the coast and still pedaling with determination. Cruising down into an unknown town at the bottom of a steep hill, Tinker forgot that on European bicycles one applied the brakes with a lever on the handle bars instead of the pedals. Suddenly two Republican militiamen appeared in the middle of the road with upraised arms and shouted "¡ALTO!" The bicycle continued on in defiance of rider and policemen, running down one guard, while his companion drew a pistol and shot the mysterious cyclist. Fortunately the bullet passed through Tinker's right side without hitting any vital organs, although he stewed for a week in a nearby hospital. His enviable record of 150 combat hours without a scratch now bowed to a trigger-happy village cop!

JULY 4TH CELEBRATION

Despite his delicate state of health, Tinker, along with Baumler and Dahl, celebrated the Fourth of July in a proper manner. The threesome collected three Very pistols together with a huge assortment of colored flares and proceeded to the main terrace of a Los Alcazares hotel. Commandeering several tables, the flyers spent the entire day sipping rum and discharging flares. At alarming intervals, the Americans would punctuate the flare salvos with nerve-shattering reports from their sidearms, followed by a few slurred bars of "The Star-Spangled Banner." Tinker recalled: "All that we lacked was an American flag to hoist. The natives, of course, thought we were hopelessly insane, but they had been of that opinion for a long time anyway. Our conduct that day merely strengthened their convictions."

BRUNETE

As Franco's North Army prepared to resume its offensive following the fall of Bilbao, the Rebels were hit by a massive attack against their lines before Madrid. The Loyalists' surprise push commenced during the night of July 5–6 and threw the Nationalist High Command into a state of near panic. The Popular Front's objectives were threefold: double envelopment of the enemy before the capital and its total destruction; severing Rebel contact with Portugal; and disruption of the northern fascist offensive. To accomplish this end, the Republic fielded between 80,000 and 90,000 troops with armor, artillery, and air power. The point of attack was a 6 mile area between the Perales and Aulencia rivers west of Madrid. Poorly defended by only several thousand Nationalist troops and a smattering of artillery, this force seemed incapable of holding the tiny hamlet of Brunete, 13 miles west of Madrid.

Franco immediately withdrew battalions and brigades from the north and other sectors and rushed them to plug the gaping holes on the Madrid front. The contest carried on through the July heat for three sultry weeks. During the fascist counteroffensive, the Condor Legion destroyed twenty-one Government planes and the Republic lost many times this number of machines to Italian and Spanish Nationalist fighters. The Red offensive was checked and held to a salient approximately a half mile deep and 10 miles wide. As before, the old stalemate resumed on the Madrid front. The Battle of Brunete accomplished nothing beyond wholesale slaughter.

On July 5, two squadrons of Moscas with Soviet pilots arrived at Barajas and Alcalá de Henares. Air historians have placed Tinker's escuadrilla at both Manzanares and Barajas during this period. A unit of Chatos with Soviet pilots replaced LaCalle's old squadron at Campo X (Azuqueca), and another I-15 group flown by Spanish pilots was based at Camposoto. Whitey Dahl was a member of this latter squadron.

Fully mended and rested, Tinker resumed escort duty for Rasante bombers, which were plastering enemy fortifications near Villa de Cañada. On July 8, during one such mission, Ajax Baumler picked off a careless Fiat pilot. The following day, Tinker's Russian squadron shepherded a dozen R-5s over to Navalcarnero southwest of Madrid. Following the bomb run, the Moscas broke away and flew to the Rebel trenches at Casa de Campo where Tinker, Baumler, and the Soviets strafed fascists until all ammunition belts were empty.

The Brunete campaign lasted three weeks during which time Tinker flew 33 missions and logged more than 37 flying hours. There he matched his skill and his I-16 against the Messerschmitt BF 109Bs of the Condor Legion, a craft he considered mediocre in combat ability. To prove his point, he shot down two of them, on July 12 and the 17, and thereby became the first American to score victories over the highly touted Messerschmitts.

FAREWELL TO WHITEY

On the evening of July 11, Tinker, Dahl, Baumler, and two Lincoln brigaders decided to gather at the Hotel Gran Via's bar. Armed with five bottles of bootlegged champagne, the party settled down to mourn Whitey's assignment to a Chato unit. The "wake" might have gone quietly except that there were five Spanish militia officers at a nearby table in the company of an equal number of beautiful señoritas. Provoked by the *extranjeros'* repeated attempts to steal their dates, the Spaniards began a five-minute brawl with their erstwhile allies. When a militiaman pulled out a pistol, the five Americans followed suit and started firing into the ceiling, whereupon the officers and their ladies took flight. Battered but unbowed, Baumler and Tinker dropped "Rubio" off at Camposoto Airfield and then proceeded to their own base at Manzanares. This memorable evening proved to be their last with Whitey Dahl.

TINKER MASTERS THE MESSERSCHMITT

Aerial action came in spades on July 12 when Tinker's escuadrilla performed escort duty for Rasantes and Katiuskas on three separate occasions and each time drew blood with enemy fighters. The Alcalá squadrons surrendered three Polikarpovs while destroying eight Fiats and one Heinkel He 51. The Italians claimed nine "kills": five Chatos and four Moscas. To Tinker's surprise, and the astonishment of the Russian pilots, the last engagement lasted well over an hour. Time permitted only the briefest realization that the Loyalist pilots were facing BF 109Bs. Three Messerschmitts jumped a Chato; before Tinker and his Soviet wingmen could assist the outmatched I-15, it had already begun its death plunge, the victim of Feldwebel Peter Boddem (who would continue to bedevil the Red Wings and record ten victories against them). Furious at himself for arriving too late to save his comrade, Tinker locked on the tail of another "Messer" (Uffz. Guido Höneß) and sent it earthward as well. Meanwhile, his Russian wingmen dispatched a second Condor Legionnaire as the third escaped. In this clash, two I-16s and Whitey Dahl's Chato went down. Tinker's log showed that twelve enemy pursuits succumbed, including several Messerschmitts, one belonging to him. The Rebel Air Force proclaimed the destruction of one I-15 and admitted the midair collision of two Fiats.

Not until Tinker landed at Barajas did he learn that Dahl had been at the controls of the ill-fated Chato he sought to rescue. Both Baumler and Tinker blamed Whitey's loss on the Air Ministry's decision to place him in an all-Spanish squadron where spoken commands were impossible for him to comprehend.

WHITEY TAKES A SECOND PLUNGE

With his Chato disabled, Dahl had tried to escape the Messerschmitts in a power dive; in the course of this maneuver, his wing collapsed. He parachuted at 5,000 feet and landed in the midst of a company of Moors. For days these African troops had been repeatedly strafed by Loyalist flyers, and they intended to vent their frustrations on their prisoner. A Spanish officer's timely arrival alone saved Whitey from being beaten to death. Taking their captive to headquarters, Dahl received food and medical attention. In his cell, however, he was intimidated with pistols and threatened with torture. The Nationalists ordered him to Salamanca where he encountered more abuse. His forthcoming execution, according to his jailers, would serve as an example to other greedy U.S. pilots.

AN INTERNATIONAL MESS

New York Times reporter William Carney, who worked the Rebel side of the war, interviewed Whitey in his Salamanca cell on July 21, and reported that the prisoner had been treated with "exquisite courtesy" by the Franco forces. Secretary of State Cordell Hull dealt himself into the growing international mess by ordering U.S. Consul George M. Graves at Vigo to confront Dahl and learn whether or not he had been illegally recruited in the United States. The foreign serviceman informed Hull on July 28 that Whitey had signed his contract to fly for the Republic in Mexico City and that the presiding judge opined that the court-martial tribunal would sentence him to death.

Meanwhile the nettlesome inmate lied when he told his captors that he held a reserve commission in the U.S. Army Air Corps. Worse still, he signed a confession accusing Captain Townsend Griffiss, the assistant military attaché in Valencia, with pro-Republican leanings. In the document, he stated that Ed Semons, the American liaison for the Loyalist government in Paris, shuttled U.S. pilots to Captain Griffiss, whose job it was to oversee matters of salary and repatriation. When challenged by the consular official, Dahl recanted his previous statement and blamed the whole incident on a misunderstanding of the prison interpreter. The hapless Griffiss was grilled by the War and State Departments in order to clarify his ties with Dahl and Semons. After much ado, the beleaguered assistant military attaché was exonerated and the whole episode was publicly dropped. Few Washington observers doubted, however, that the Roosevelt administration would eventually revenge itself on Dahl and his ilk.

TINKER SUFFERS BATTLE FATIGUE

As the Brunete show wore on, almost the last of the seasoned Soviet aviators were rotated back home; consequently there were not enough Russian veterans to assume leadership roles. Under these circumstances, Tinker agreed to command a squadron of Red Moscas in the air with the understanding that a Soviet C.O. would both fly with him and assume charge on the ground. Although this arrangement was nothing new to him, his having served in a similar capacity in the Spanish Air Force, still he took comfort in the certainty that never again would a U.S. Naval Academy midshipman be likely to lead a squadron of the Russian Air Force into battle.

For Tinker, the Brunete tour was particularly arduous. All pilots were required to be at the airfield before dawn's early light, and there was no respite until night. There was air cover to be flown during infantry offensives, bombers and ground-attack planes required fighter protection, and incessant air raid alarms of incoming enemy bomber forays, many of them false, frazzled his nerves. Without the deployment of radar, air raid alerts were determined by visual contact and conveyed by telephone. Sundown gave no assurance that the base was safe from attack; nocturnal aerial bombardment compromised everyone's sleep. During the aerial bombardment of Campo Real airstrip, an Italian bomb landed 15 feet from Gregoric, a Russian motor technician. The blast tore a huge hole in the man's side. When he discovered the extent of the damage by fumbling around with his right hand, the mechanic drew his pistol and shot himself. Barbaric scenes of this sort took its toll on Tinker's otherwise tranquil nature. Also, Baumler's hospitalization for a throat infection depressed him further, especially during a time when he chafed under the weight of command. The Soviet replacements were friendly enough, but they spoke no Spanish and Tinker's use of Russian was limited to the cockpit. With Ajax in a Valencia infirmary, he could no longer enjoy the free-and-easy association of a fellow American.

The Russians awarded Tinker with another three-flight day on July 14, despite his personal angst. The ensuing day was busier still. Exhausted from three earlier sorties of the day, he got orders late in the afternoon to ferry eighteen Rasantes over the lines to Brunete. As usual, the I-16s veered off to Casa de Campo after the bombardment for a bit of ground strafing. As soon as Tinker's airmen arrived on the scene, they were attacked by a bevy of Fiats and Heinkel He 51s. Fortune smiled again, however, and a half hour and eleven destroyed fascist planes later, he landed at Barajos. Tinker stood down on July 16; and with no missions to undertake, he had an opportunity to bid Ajax a fond farewell.

TINKER DOWNS ANOTHER "MESSER"

The next day, July 17, came with more escort duty and more dogfights. It also gave Tinker a chance to inspect the fighting capability of the Messerschmitt more closely. He discovered that the BF 109 could outdive the I-16 and that it possessed a superior engine. Conversely, the Mosca was faster on the straightaway and could outclimb and outmaneuver its German counterpart. The perceptive Tinker was well versed in this critical information when he slipped behind a "Messer" as it prepared to assail a patrol of Chatos. As he recalled the incident in his book, *Some Still Live*: "Aware of his danger, he (the German pilot) pulled up and tried a climbing turn—which was a fatal error. I tacked onto his tail and played my machine guns like an accordion. His motor finally burst flames and the pilot took to his parachute." What a day! Tinker's Reds flamed one Junker bomber, two He 51s, and two BF 109s. The Republican flyers lost one Chato, a fair exchange, mused the Arkansan, considering that the Condor Legion had thrown its best against them. Tinker noticed a few Fiats high above this engagement, but he dismissed the Italians as nothing more than curious observers. He had about as much respect for his German adversaries as he had contempt for their allies, the Regia Aeronautica.

TINKER'S LAST KILL

July 18 marked the beginning of the Nationalist counter offensive at Brunete. Aerial activity became intense with five major clashes. The Fiats claimed 8 Natacha bombers, one of which was destroyed by García Morato; a BF109 and a CR 32 fell that day. Tinker's squadron pulled escort duty on three occasions and dogfought the Rebels during each sortie. On his last flight, he was assailed by what seemed to be the entire fascist air service. The air reverberated with the sounds of straining engines and the staccato of machine guns for some 25 miles, a stretch from Madrid to El Escorial. Tinker flushed a Fiat under the base of a pancake-shaped cumulus cloud. The Insurgent flyer realized instantly that the monoplane he faced could outclimb him, so he executed a half roll and went into a vertical dive. Tinker's speedier Mosca almost caused him to overshoot his quarry as the I-16's guns stitched the CR 32 from rudder to cowling, killing its pilot in mid-journey. It gave Tinker a rush to see his eighth "kill" explode into the ground. Although he disliked strafing Rebel infantry and regarded the practice as a form of poaching, it never for an instant bothered him to consider the awful terror of those enemy airmen who died by his hand in their confining metal coffins, strapped in, and in terrible mental and physical agony. Victory and defeat, life and death, went with the territory. He banged the side of his seat with boyish enthusiasm. One suspects that Tinker's service was no longer a question of bonus money; rather, it was a matter of personal achievement, employer satisfaction, and, more important, the defense of a demonstratively superior political alternative to fascism.

Before sunrise on July 20, three formations of Junkers Ju 52s bombed Alcalá. Tinker and his Russian wingmen took to the sky in pursuit of the bombers. They ran the fascists all the way to Guadalajara, but failed to bring them down. However, as the I-16s fired continuously at the Junkers, one developed a smoking engine, suggesting that it was on the verge of catching fire. The rear machine gunner, believing his machine to be afire, proceeded to jump and tried to activate his parachute. Unfortunately he pulled the rip-cord too soon, and the chute caught on the bomber's tail assembly. The last Tinker saw of the enemy plane it was headed down in a long shallow dive toward its own lines with the gunner still dangling helplessly from the tail surfaces.

Despite his brilliant career in Spain, Tinker realized that his nerves were frayed. Toward the end of his tour, he intercepted and nearly opened fire on a twin-engine bomber until, right before he tripped his guns, he identified his intended prey as a Russian SB-2 Katiuska of the People's Air Force. This near tragedy persuaded him to leave the service. That evening, after a day of five missions totaling more than five hours of flying, Tinker wrote to the Air Ministry giving them the required ten-day notice for termination of his contract. He continued flying regularly with the Soviets until July 29, when he made his last flight in Spain.

7

MUSTERING OUT

> For the benefit of those readers who might think it unpatriotic to use training given by this Government [US] in fighting for a foreign Government I will add that I had offered my services to this country long before leaving for Spain. Also, if they care to examine the army files in Washington, they will find that I have lodged another formal offer of my services to the U. S. Army Air Corps, since my return. The Air Corps doesn't seem to be interested, however, so I suppose there is nothing left except to follow Horace Greeley's advice and go West. [veiled reference to Claire Chennault's "Flying Tigers" and his service in China]
>
> Concluding paragraph of Frank Tinker's *Some Still Live*

On July 30, the Russian regional commander called from Alcalá to inform Tinker that he would spend a few days in Valencia prior to his separation. In the interim, a new Soviet flyer was sent to relieve his American comrade. After a week at Alcalá, Tinker arrived in Valencia for a week's layover prior to his departure for Barcelona. Purely by chance, he met his old wingman, Manuel Gomez, who had been shot down and captured by the Rebels on March 20. The Guatemalan mercenary had languished in a Salamanca prison for four months before being traded to the Republicans for an Italian pilot. Gomez's tale of starvation and poor medical attention at the hands of the fascists, coupled with the flyer's badly burned left hand, left Tinker in a state of depression. For some time after their meeting, the Arkansan could still hear his old squadronmate's hollow assurances that he would fly combat again.

GOING HOME

By August 15, Baumler had completed his plans for returning to the United States. As in the case of many "volunteers," he owned an American passport, but the document stated that it was invalid for travel in Spain. As "Ajax's" passport carried two visas in it attesting to the fact that he had entered Spain, remained there seven months, and then left, he elected to return home in a roundabout way. The flyer boarded a Canadian-Pacific liner bound for Canada. From there, Baumler simply flew into the United States aboard a military transport plane.

On August 12, Tinker's train departed from Barcelona for Port Bou on the Franco-Spanish border. Despite a brief misunderstanding with French police in Perpignan, he obtained a safe-conduct pass for Paris. Once there, he spent nine frustrating days trying to secure an American visa on his Spanish passport. Finally, the vice-consul agreed to grant him a U.S. passport providing he secured positive identification from a fellow countryman. Tinker headed for Harry's New York Bar, a prominent watering hole for visiting Americans in Paris. Regrettably, his first encounter was with an old enemy, Vincent Minor Schmidt, another mercenary in Paris who would fly a contraband Vultee V1A to Barcelona within days. When Schmidt attempted to extract a "loan" from his former flying partner, Tinker walked away. Later he angrily explained to a friend at the bar that Schmidt had run from a fight. It seemed that his long-lost comrade had been flying Breguets with him in January 1937, and that on one sortie Schmidt had deserted the Arkansan in the face of enemy fire.

As the prospect of a barroom brawl evaporated, Tinker spotted his old host at Madrid's Hotel Florida. Hemingway certified Tinker's identity, and he secured his passport on August 25. However, the U.S. consulate awarded the passport to the purser of the liner *Champlain* with the understanding that it would be presented to a State Department representative once the ship arrived in the United States. Tinker boarded the *Champlain* at La Havre under guard. When he arrived in New York City, a State Department official interrogated him for hours about the military situation in Spain. Tinker confided to his one-man welcoming committee that he suffered from shell shock and that further questioning might result in an emotional outburst. He lied about staying at the Commodore Hotel, and once the government official was out of sight, he took lodgings in Jersey City. Having satisfied several long-standing social obligations in the area, Tinker headed south for his hometown of DeWitt.

THE END OF THE BEGINNING

The Republic's air force fought on without Tinker and its other American eagles. Their departure, however, seemed to produce a domino effect of military stalemates and disasters. In the north, Santander fell on August 26 and Gijon surrendered on October 21. Franco now held all of northern Spain with its vital resources and two-thirds of the country. On March 9, 1938, Franco's armies launched a major offensive in Aragon, driving back the Republican defenders and reaching the Mediterranean coast by the middle of April. This military thrust opened an 80 mile wide corridor between Catalonia and the southern zone of the Republic. In France, newly reelected Premier León Blum relaxed frontier restrictions for the free flow of arms to the Loyalists, but he was obliged by the British to close it again on June 13.

Back in Arkansas, Tinker undertook the defense of the Republic and its air service in an autobiographical account. Consulting a daily calendar he kept while in Spain, Tinker managed to flesh out his story, supplementing the chronicle with facts from his flight diary. His efforts resulted in a book entitled *Some Still Live*, which was published in August 1938 in the United States, England, and Sweden. Segments of the work had been serialized earlier in four April issues of *The Saturday Evening Post.* On May 5, 1938, Hemingway wrote editor Maxwell Perkins about the counterfeits and heroes in his Spanish Civil War NANA dispatches, concluding: "When finished am going to settle down and write about the pricks and fakers like [André] Malraux who pulled out in February '37 to write gigantic masterpisses before it really started, will have a good lesson when write ordinary sized book with the old stuff unfaked in it. What stuff there is. Did you read Frank Tinker's articles in the *Post*? Satevepost? They were damned good." Reviewer David Garrett wrote of *Some Still Live* for *The New Statesman and Nation*:

> It is a simple book, not well written, by a man who is not good at analyzing his feelings, or describing his emotions. But the things he does say carry one a long way.... Like so many tough Americans, Tinker becomes capable of introspection and tenderness, when describing drinking and girls, but is not good at describing moments of fear. Yet I suppose that like other pilots his knees have sometimes gone out of control after landing, so that he has had to push his legs straight with his hand before he could use [the] rudder, taxying. ... *Some Still Live* is a book everyone

interested in Spain, in flying, *and in what is coming to us,* should read.

In August, following the publication of his book, Tinker canoed down the White River into the Arkansas River, and finally reached the Mississippi. His sole companion on this trip was his pet fox Susie. While en route, Tinker drafted a series of articles for a Little Rock newspaper. Hollywood saw his book's promise and offered to produce a motion picture based on Tinker's story, but he lacked the will to pursue the initiative. Still, his attention never deviated from the Republic's desperate struggle back in Spain, and he followed the civil war as closely as the local media permitted.

THE BEGINNING OF THE END

Inside that war-torn nation, the beginning of the Popular Front's end was about to unfold. On July 13, 1938, a combined Nationalist force attacked south from Teruel. The front was driven back 56 miles along an 18 mile line.

The Battle of the Ebro represented a last-ditch attempt by the Republicans to reunite the two halves of the Government's former territory divided during the Aragon campaign, or failing that, at least to insure the survival of its regime until the anticipated outbreak of World War II, which might perhaps save it from certain defeat. The Loyalist offensive began on July 24–25, with an assault force of four army corps crossing the Ebro River. The Rebels hit back with airpower in an attempt to straighten the enemy salient, while regrouping to launch their own counterattack. Franco scotched the Government's drive on August 2, 1938, and four days later inaugurated his own offensive.

Between the middle of July and the middle of September, the Morato groups of 2-G-3 and 3-G-3 destroyed 44 enemy aircraft. Since their inception, the two Spanish Nationalist Fiat groups had accounted for 151 Government machines downed, and Morato's personal score amounted to 34 victories. In early August, his Fiat groups were involved in intermittent air clashes over the River Zújar Cabeza de Buey sector, dogfights that became ever more contentious as the month progressed. Red Wings seemed to keep their distance as Rebel machines ravaged targets along the Ebro loop. During early October, the Morato Fiat groups fought side by side accounting for 25 "kills" between them. In these air battles, the Italian Gamba de Ferro group and the Russian squadrons no.2 and no. 5 fought for the last time.

From October 30 until November 3, there were six major air engagements in which the Morato groups shot down 30 more enemy planes without a single loss. On November 2 the two groups participated in a veritable turkey shoot, destroying seven Red Wings in the morning and ten more in the afternoon. The Condor Legion now began receiving cannon-firing BF109 "Es," and its company turned over the outdated "Bs" to Spanish Nationalist pilots. Also during this phase of action, a new Morato group was created: 5-G-5. This group, together with 2-G-3 and 3-G-3, became the 7th Fighter Squadron with Morato as its commander.

DISENGAGEMENT

On October 15, 10,000 Italians embarked at Cadiz for home. In less than two weeks, approximately 3,500 Internationals who fought for the Republic left Barcelona. As a gesture of farewell, one hundred Loyalist fighters flew over Ciudad Condal to protect them from Rebel attack. The Soviets, too, were abandoning Spain. Following the Munich Crisis, a Russo-German accord was in the offing. Also, the purge of 1937 had made it inadvisable for highly placed military and civilian officers and officials to travel abroad. Moreover, Stalin saw the war as lost; he did not want more Russian flyers to be taken prisoner.

TINKER IN EXILE

As his depression deepened over the plight of the Spanish Republic and his own forced inactivity, Tinker threatened to fly a plane nonstop across the Atlantic to Spain, but the State Department alerted the Civil Aeronautics Authority to arrest him if he attempted the flight. The Departments of War and State abruptly rejected his application for the post of air attaché in Spain.

Al Baumler's visit to DeWitt hoisted Tinker's spirits during this time. "Ajax's" military career had suffered no reversals as a consequence of his service in Spain inasmuch as he was flying with the Army Air Corps. Adding insult to injury, Baumler told his old comrade that he might enlist in a new international group of mercenary fighter pilots being organized to fight the Japanese in China. Tinker appreciated his friend's need for an assignment and his appetite for action, but he himself preferred to return to Spain and fight for the Republic. His sense of remorsefulness had nothing to do with his having flown for money, but rather to do with his having returned home too soon, having abandoned an ideal for the sake of personal loneliness and fatigue. Could he have made a difference in the air war there;

and, if not, should he have remained to fly and die, if not together with his former comrades, at least with those who now carried the war to the enemy?

What had his Spanish tour of duty meant to Tinker on a psychological level? It had meant a new direction and meter in his life: the satisfaction of former missions well performed and the imperative of the next one only hours away; it had meant both he and his comrades at their best carrying death and destruction to the opposition and enduring the same in equal measure; it had meant a sense of involvement, if not belonging—a kind of martial brotherhood—never imagined by him. He was genuinely inspired by what he believed to be a righteous cause against a hateful enemy, to be sure; but could he live without the life-sustaining, kinetic force of conflict? In Tinker's view, the survival of the Republic would validate not only his contributions and sacrifices in Spain, but also who and what he had become; its demise, conversely, would repudiate the most defining phase of his young life. He could not disengage himself from the fate of a dying government.

FINALE

On November 26, 1938, eight days after the end of the Ebro campaign, Franco ordered an attack in Catalonia to commence on December 10. The caudillo split his force into five Spanish corps of three divisions each, plus an Italian corps of four divisions. This army opposed twenty Government divisions, all of which were at one-half to one-third their original size. In the skies, Messerschmitts dominated the battlefield.

On Christmas Eve, Morato's 3-G-3 group downed nine Red Natacha bombers, of which Morato claimed three. On December 28, the Italian As de Bastos group destroyed 14 Chatos in exchange for a single Fiat, and several days thereafter its sister group, La Cucaracha, flamed 10 Loyalist machines, again for the loss of a single CR 32.

With the taking of Tarragona on January 14, 1939, and Barcelona on the 26th, Condor Legion pilots were unleashed to destroy targets of opportunity across the coastal plain of Catalonia. Messerschmitts strafed bedraggled supply lines, sank transports, and otherwise harried the rear echelons of a retreating army. Republican aircraft were in harm's way, both on the ground and in the air. Almost symbolically, Morato's final dogfight occurred at Iqualada on January 19 where he downed an I-15, bringing his final score to 40 victories.

On February 27, Great Britain and France extended diplomatic recognition to Franco, which prompted the resignation of exiled President Manuel Azaña. Minister of Defense Dr. Juan Negrín assumed control of the government and placed a dispirited and crumbling army under pro-Communist Colonel Juan Modesto. This action resulted in calls for Negrín's resignation from within the Popular Front government. On March 5, the Loyalist Navy mutinied and sailed to Algiers. Open fighting erupted in the streets of Madrid between the Communists and dissidents who called for an end to the fighting. The Condor Legion bombed Madrid, Toledo, and Valencia as a way to force the government's surrender. Toledo capitulated, and the Republican forces were in full retreat. By March 27, white flags were draped from hundreds of balconies in Madrid. The Popular Front government fell on March 29, 1939.

A film was being produced at Seville on April 4 concerning the exploits of the Condor Legion. In one of the sequences, a dogfight was to be reenacted involving a BF 109, a Mosca, a Chato, and a Fiat, Morato's legendary "3-51." The filming had concluded, and Morato, in high spirits over the outcome of the war, gave an unrehearsed show of aerobatics. He dived, leveled out, and skimmed the ground at full throttle, then went into a steep climb, rolling as the plane nosed higher into the sky. At the apex of his climb, the Fiat stalled and spun earthward. On April 5, the senior officers of the Fiat groups accompanied Morato's body to his hometown of Málaga where, on April 6, he was laid to rest, his burial attended by nearly everyone in the town. A monolith was subsequently erected at the crash site, and the group's old Blue Patrol badge was chiseled out of the rough granite. Eleven years after his death, Franco titled Morato the Count of Jarama in recognition of his contributions to the Nationalist cause.

On May 22, fascist Spain bade farewell to the Condor Legion at Leon. The Legionary Air Force moved to Tablada on May 30, where it transferred all aircraft and equipment to the Spaniards. Shortly thereafter, this expeditionary force embarked at Cadiz, bound for Genoa. At last, Francisco Franco owned Spain!

TINKER'S SUICIDE

On June 13, Tinker sat oblivious to the dinginess of his surroundings in Little Rock's Hotel Ben McGhee, occasionally glimpsing a nearby .22 caliber revolver through an alcoholic haze, his reverie cruelly framed by this eighth and last night as a guest. Scattered about the spartan room were relics of his derring-do career with La Patrulla Americana. A bottle of scotch at hand would help measure his noctural musings and remind him of his awful resolve at dawn. Beside the whiskey lay a letter of acceptance from the Chinese Air Force, the result of ongoing correspondence between Tinker and General Claire Chennault in Hankow.

His unceremonious end proved to be as controversial as his brief twenty-nine years of life. The medical examiners and the military establishment attributed the shooting to a case of shell shock. Back in Arkansas, however, friends and neighbors dismissed this theory as poppycock, insisting that Frank would never employ a "varmint" pistol when he had packed a .45 Colt automatic in his suitcase. The folks in his hometown of DeWitt compromised on the engraving emblazoned on his tombstone: "¿Quien Sabe?"

In late July 1939, Hemingway learned from a correspondent in Arkansas that Frank Tinker had apparently committed suicide. The writer replied that he would have tried to dissuade his comrade from taking his life had he known about the flyer's condition. Hemingway confessed that he had frequently argued himself out of suicidal impulses. The trick, he confided, was not to allow discouragement to tempt one into taking the easy way out.

In a measured way, Papa had seen in Tinker's brief life the stuff of legend, and he mourned both his mortal death and his passing as a Hemingway hero. How he detested the architects of America's Non-Intervention laws in Washington and abroad, those who had denied his comrade the chance to resume his crusade in Spain and thereby serve mankind; still, he could not condone the young man's suicide. Had Tinker forgotten the magical symbiosis of life and struggle, a lesson so aptly taught in Spain? As the civil war progressed, the writer had applauded Tinker's budding faith in the Republic as the flyer's acceptance of a transcendent ideal worthy of his defense and his life. For Hemingway, however, the key to Tinker's character was his ability to walk that tightrope between one's exposure to the brutalization of war and the simple faith of his Arkansas roots—a mental and moral equilibrium which allowed him to serve both as a paid mercenary and a genuine hero of the Republican cause.

8

LIFE AND DEATH AFTER SPAIN

> They were the last of the knight errant, of the cavaliers of a new Roncesvalles. They clung to a single touch of chivalry that had been forgotten in the welter of treason, butchery, and betrayal. Like the heroic warriors of Roland, each left his mark after fighting against great odds.
>
> Arthur H. Landis
> *The Abraham Lincoln Brigade*

Ben Leider's eventual return to the United States had been long anticipated and heralded with much fanfare. A memorial service was held on April 26, 1937, at the New York City Hippodrome with 2,500 spectators in attendance. Rabbi Stephen S. Wise, Representative John T. Bernard of Minnesota, and Angelo Herndon, darling of the American Communist Party whose Georgia conviction on an antebellum anti-insurrection law had been overturned that same day by the U.S. Supreme Court, were among the speakers. Everyone urged support of the Republic as a means of honoring Leider's sacrifice. During the following sixteen months, there were numerous rallies, marches, fund-raisers, memorials, articles, and left-wing pulp biographies to sustain the memory of the slain Jewish volunteer.

In mid-July 1938, Leider's body was exhumed from the municipal cemetery at Colmenar de Oreja, outside Madrid, near the site of his fatal crash, and placed aboard the British steamer *Fredavore* on August 1 for Marseille, where it was transferred to a New York-bound vessel. For the past thirteen months, the Loyalist martyr's grave had become a virtual shrine, and it had been the custom for Government pilots taking off on missions at a nearby aerodrome to salute this hallowed plot.

On the evening of August 18, the funeral cortège of Ben Leider passed through Times Square on its way to Carnegie Hall. A huge guard of honor comprising 125 veterans of the Abraham Lincoln Battalion were in uniform filing along with members of patriotic, civic, and fraternal groups sympathetic to the Spanish Republic, together with 2,000 mourners. Led by a small band of men in khaki-and-blue overseas caps, who were beating muffled drums, the cortège turned north at Broadway and Forty-fifth Street and marched slowly to Carnegie Hall for a memorial meeting. A throng of 5,000 persons encircled the hall as the procession arrived about 8:00 p.m.

The Carnegie Hall stage was banked with flowers against a backdrop of black-and-purple streamers and the interlinked flags of the United States and Republican Spain. The coffin was carried to the stage between rows of International Brigaders who stood at salute. The Reverend Benjamin Plotkin of Congregation Emann-El of Jersey City told the 3,000 faithful in the hall that Leider was "no mere adventurer, no conventional hero, but a soldier of a new time who, loving humanity and sensitive to its sufferings, was glad to sacrifice his life for a noble cause." "When the war came to Spain," continued Plotkin, "when again, as in his childhood he heard the screams of mothers and children, as death came tearing down from the skies, his heart was touched." Plotkin's words cascaded over the audience as he thundered: "This was no ordinary war; this was an attack upon humanity itself. Savages had fallen upon a land, ready to destroy a whole population. And resistance in his mind meant a definite thing—turning back the enemy with weapons in your hands."

Other speakers included the president of Leider's beloved New York Newspaper Guild, two war correspondents, a poet, a representative of the Abraham Lincoln Battalion, and Dr. William Leider, a brother. Leider was buried on August 21, 1938, in the Mount Hebron Cemetery, Flushing, New York, in the presence of 300 of his kith and kin. As those in attendance paid their final respects, who among them could have known that World War II was only 375 days away?

For the remaining seventeen years of his beleaguered life, Bert Acosta endured intermittent bouts with alcohol and child support suits from an irate ex-spouse. The last time he climbed into a cockpit was in Texas in 1946 where he appeared at a farewell dinner for General Henry H. (Hap) Arnold on his retirement as Air Force chief. It became known that Acosta was living in Garrison, New York, with the Catholic Fathers of the Atonement, who ran St. Christopher's Inn for homeless men at their monastery, Graymoor. There he worked in the carpenter shop and sang in the friar's guest choir.

Back on the street, broke and alone, Acosta collapsed in New York City in 1952. Admiral Richard Byrd learned of his old friend's plight and raised money to send him to a sanitarium out west. Acosta lingered for two years before his death from tuberculosis in the Jewish Consumptive Relief Society's nonsectarian sanitarium near Denver, Colorado. Flying comrade George Noville flew up from California just days before Acosta's death on September 1, 1954. The frail aerial legend extracted from Noville his promise to fulfill a dying man's final request, to have his ashes scattered over the Pacific off the California coast.

Back in the United States, Charlie Koch regained his health and returned to work at his former profession, aircraft design and engineering. In 1937–38, Koch worked for the Canadian Car and Foundry Corporation designing the Grumman FF-1, a two-seat biplane fighter. By chance, he discovered that these planes had been previously manufactured by Grumman for the U.S. Navy and were now being "laundered" through his firm and sent to Spain. Despite his association with the Spanish Republic, Koch quit his job, not wishing to be a part of this subterfuge. In time, the FF-1s were shipped to Spain. Koch's first fighter commander, Andrés LaCalle, led a squadron of these pursuits late in the war. Following a "cup of coffee" with his old employer, the Seversky Corporation, Koch moved on to the Barkley-Grow Aircraft Corporation in Detroit, Michigan. There he remained from early 1938 until November 1940, designing commercial airliners.

As war raged in Europe, the necessity for mass produced aircraft became evident; consequently the automobile industry and the federal government created an advisory body called the Automotive Committee for Air Defense (ACAD). Organized to educate the automobile manufacturers on the intricacies of building planes and headed by Jimmy Doolittle, the nation's car builders were persuaded to assume the responsibility of constructing aircraft. Koch was asked to serve as the group's technical advisor.

When automobile manufacturer Henry Ford reentered the aircraft construction business, the ACAD assisted the corporation. Ford management chose to build the Consolidated-Vultee B24 bomber, and Koch was invited by Ford executives to participate in this enterprise. On the heels of his contributions to the establishment of the production line in a huge new plant at Willow Run, Michigan, Koch ran afoul of Ford management and returned to New York City in June 1944. From this point until his final retirement in 1973, Koch was associated with three additional aircraft-related corporations. He lived another decade, dying on September 5, 1983.

Albert Baumler attended New York University for a year after his tour in

Spain while maintaining contact with Tinker. Over a period of time, he helped his squadronmate in a lawsuit brought about by fellow flyer O. D. Bell. When *The Saturday Evening Post* published its "Some Still Live" series based on Tinker's book, Bell read the installments and went berserk. In his articles, Tinker bluntly asserted that Bell had failed his flight checks and was summarily shipped back to the States. Bell's ire stemmed from a dubious story of his own Spanish exploits which he sold to several magazines following his tour of duty. His rage manifested itself in lawsuits against both Tinker and the *Saturday Evening Post*.

"O.D." received support from Derek Dickinson, whom Tinker also wrote in his book was found to be unacceptable as a pursuit pilot. According to the author, Dickinson's age alone, estimated by Tinker to be around forty, would have barred him from fighter service. Actually, Dickinson remained with the Air Ministry for nearly fourteen months, longer than any other American volunteer. From December 1936 until midsummer 1937, Dickinson flew reconnaissance, fulfilling the remainder of his contractual obligations in the area of aviation mechanics. He, too, had peddled some remarkable stories to "action" magazines.

Once back home, Dickinson recounted to a *Herald Tribune* reporter his account of an air duel with Bruno Mussolini, the Duce's youngest son. The contest reputedly took place on September 28, 1937. Dickinson claimed that both he and Mussolini flew monoplanes (I-16 and a Fiat G 50) and that each pilot had two observation planes in tow as witnesses. The Spanish subsecretary of Air, Augustin Sanz Sainz, honored Dickinson by serving as one of his observers. The early phases of the dogfight resulted in a draw, claimed the American, until he circled behind the Italian and opened fire; whereupon Mussolini signaled his surrender. Dickinson told reporters that he ended the battle and returned to base. Perhaps the most bizarre tale to emerge from the Spanish Civil War, Dickinson sold the account to *For Men* magazine and later condensed for *Reader's Digest*.

In addition to the contemporary statements by Tinker, Baumler, and other volunteer pilots concerning Dickinson's penchant for exaggeration, aviation historians have since branded this chronicle as rubbish. First, Bruno Mussolini arrived in Spain in late September 1937 as a bomber pilot. He subsequently participated in twenty-seven sorties in a Savoia-Marchetti SM 79 and returned to Italy in March 1938, reportedly because the Republican Air Ministry had put a bounty on his head. Second, his alledged fighter, the Fiat G 50, was the sole Italian monoplane to appear in Spain, and it did not debut until January 1939. At the time of the so-called duel, there were only two prototypes in existence. Third, Dickinson's primary witness,

Sanz Sainz, who commanded the airfield at Alcalá de Henares, had perished in a bombing raid six months prior to the Dickinson-Mussolini aerial engagement (March 23, 1937).

Baumler came to Tinker's defense, and the suit was dropped. Following Tinker's death, Bell renewed the lawsuit against his detractor's estate and won an insignificant sum for his trouble. Shortly after the Japanese attack on Pearl Harbor, Bell applied for duty with the American Air Force and in March 1943, was commissioned a captain and assigned to the U.S. Army Ferry Command. Five months later he died of a heart attack at forty-six years of age.

Ajax Baumler went to China in 1941 to obtain a contract. Despite the fact that his quest ended in failure, he did participate in a few raids with Claire Chennault's American Volunteer Group (AVG). When the AVG became the 23rd Fighter group of the United States Army Air Force in 1942, Baumler joined as an officer pilot. With the end of World War II and the onset of the cold war, Baumler served as GCA controller in Korea. It is the irony of history that had Baumler been young enough during this "police action," he might have flown against some of the Russian aviators who were his comrades in Spain.

After seven months in the United States, Vincent Joseph Patriarca secured a new Italian passport on July 20, 1937, and sailed for Italy to enlist in the Italian Air Force. Soon thereafter Secretary of State Cordell Hull learned that Patriarca had migrated to Spain and was once again flying with the Regia Aeronautica. This bothersome expatriate survived the Spanish Civil War and subsequently flew for Il Duce in North Africa during World War II. Patriarca ended his career in Naples as an employee of the U.S. Navy.

On August 17, 1937, four Vultee V1A fighters were flown out of Paris to Toulouse en route to Republican Spain. Tinker's old nemesis, Vincent Minor Schmidt, piloted one of the aircraft to Barcelona, where he delivered it to the Loyalist government. Despite Tinker's low opinion of his former flying comrade, Schmidt enjoyed a solid reputation in Air Ministry circles. Earlier in the civil war he had flown night bombing missions out of Alicante and Barcelona. On a particular nocturnal sortie he took the place of a Spanish pilot who refused to man a bomb-laden craft without adequate runway lighting. Schmidt not only accomplished the mission, but landed his bomber with only the assistance of car headlights as beacons. He survived the Spanish Civil War to command the 14th Volunteer (bombardment) Squadron in China in 1938. Also in the squadron was James "Tex" Allison, Tinker's old comrade from La Patrulla Americana days. Schmidt next migrated to Finland in 1939–40 to fly with an international squadron against the Soviets. Hostilities ended before Schmidt got airborne, however, and all he accrued from the campaign was frostbitten feet.

For a time, there was great confusion as to whether Harold Dahl would be tried by the Spanish Nationalists as a war criminal or paroled as a prisoner of war. Then, on September 27, 1937, the Rebels set his trial date for October 3. Whitey took it all in stride: " . . . military court . . . Tried and convicted, I was assured by my cheery guards! And the charges? Here's where you get a laugh! We were charged with "taking up arms against the Spanish Government." Can you match that for sheer ironical effrontery? A charge like that brought by a bunch of revolutionists who were engaged themselves in an attempt to overthrow that same government."

Franco put Whitey on public display in a courtroom packed with reporters. In order to milk the proceedings of its entertainment value, the fascists tried Dahl along with three Russian and three Spanish Republican aviators. The American drew a public defender, the Marqués del Merito, who even met with El Caudillo in Burgos. The military court, comprised of nine officers in their natty uniforms, returned a predictable verdict of guilty, and Dahl was scheduled for execution at 6:00 a.m. on October 8.

Edith Dahl hoped to save Whitey's life and spark her own career. She wrote Franco:

> I am writing to explain that my husband Harold Dahl is politically neutral. He joined the Spanish government air force only because there are too many aviators in the U.S. We have been married only eight months. I'm all alone. He flew only to get money for me. I know you are a man with a great heart and much courage. I give you my word that Harold will not fight you again if you have the compassion to give him his freedom and send him back to me now. Now that victory is almost within your grasp, the life of one American pilot cannot mean much to you. I was an actress for several years but only now have I found my happiness. Don't destroy it. Please answer my letter so I may know what to do and if I can hope.

Edith sent along a fetching snapshot of herself in a clinging bathing suit to the Generalissimo. A week later, Franco's nephew called and informed her that "Whitey's" life would be spared and that he would be included in the next prisoner exchange. Franco's namesake invited Edith to join his uncle until her husband's release. She thanked him, but deferred, preferring to wait for Whitey in Cannes. Dahl's imprisonment continued, while his wife appeared in Parisian nightclubs billed as "the woman who melted Franco's heart." On the eve of his being shot, Dahl heard an unruly mob streaming down the jail corridor, shouting: "Whitey"! Old Boy, you've been pardoned! There'll be no execution!" Beaming reporters ran up to shake his hand.

The three Soviet flyers had their sentences reduced to life imprisonment and were exchanged soon thereafter. Time passed, and while the Republic swapped German and Italian airmen for Russian aviators, Dahl was passed over perhaps due to rumors that he offered to fly for Franco, reports which he vehemently denied. Whitey obtained a parole on October 10, 1937, and received a private room in the officer's section of the military hospital at Salamanca after his promise not to escape. By now he enjoyed the run of Salamanca during daylight and the right to receive funds from abroad. Whitey was released on February 22, 1940, and returned to America on the *SS Exiria* on March 17 with the next-to-last batch of homebound prisoners.

The press hailed Dahl's arrival in New York City on March 17, 1940. A full half hour later, his wife pulled up in a black limousine flanked by male escorts. As the couple hugged before popping cameras, Edith whispered, "Don't smear my lipstick, Whitey. You'll ruin the pictures." Five minutes after the final photo, she climbed into the limo and sped away leaving Whitey behind. Following several months of rest and relaxation, Dahl departed for Canada and a commission in the Royal Canadian Air Force (RCAF). Before leaving, however, Whitey was arrested again for passing rubber checks. He was freed when the presiding judge happened to be a congenial fellow member of the Quiet Birdmen, an aviators' association.

Dahl posted an enviable record with the Royal Canadian Air Force during World War II and even remarried. Whenever questions arose about his former marriage, Whitey suggested that he had never been legally hitched. At war's end, however, Whitey was cashiered for peddling RCAF equipment, which had not been declared surplus. With a family to support, he found work in Venezuela and then with a commercial airline, Swissair, flying the Geneva-to-Paris route. For a time, Dahl kept himself in check in spite of frequent bouts with boredom. Regrettably, this tranquil phase of his life abruptly ended on October 5, 1953, when a bar of gold bullion valued at $35,000 vanished from the cargo hold of a plane Dahl flew from Paris to Geneva. Subsequent reports put the fugitive, along with a former Swissair stewardess, at Monte Carlo, at Cannes, in Rome, and in Vichy. At Paris' Hotel Ritz, an alert house detective arrested the elusive couple. Whitey's girlfriend produced an alibi the night of the gold theft and won her release, leaving Dahl in the lurch.

Whitey languished in prison for months awaiting trial. When he finally appeared in court, the jury rejected his contention that the small fortune discovered in his hotel room came from gambling. His sentence amounted to several years in prison, a decade's banishment from Switzerland, and the payment of court costs. The authorities desired to see the last of Dahl; so he was allowed his freedom during appeal and encouraged to leave Switzerland. Whitey headed straight for Canada. Despite his age, he took a job as a bush pilot flying supplies to Arctic radar sites. At Frobisher Bay on Baffin Island, the proprietor of an overworked DC-3 employed Dahl to ferry several passengers back to the mainland. Whitey was only minutes away from his destination when his plane malfunctioned on February 14, 1956. The wreckage of his last, fatal crash was located northwest of Fort Chimo at the head of Ungara Bay, 800 miles north of Quebec.

Edith Rogers Dahl went to Australia in 1959 with a revue company, "Ziegfeld Follies," and settled down in Sydney working the night club circuit and ship cruises. She died on November 17, 1985, at the age of eighty-one, always remembered as "The Blonde Who Spiked the Guns of General Franco's Firing Squad."

EPILOGUE

The Spanish Republic's recruitment of American flyers during the early phase of the civil war proved to be an invaluable propaganda device which far exceeded the actual military contributions of these men. The presence of the September and November enlistees, despite their uneven performances, was the necessary link between Malraux's Escadre España and the arrival of the Soviet air contingent. Once on the line around Madrid and in the north, these men helped to promote worldwide public awareness of the Republic's Popular Front struggle against Franco and his proxies.

On balance, the December arrivals were the most effective flyers because they were not unduly influenced by the outmoded training and aerial experiences of the Great War (it is doubtful that veteran Bell flew combat in Spain), and World War I flight instructor Koch kept abreast as an aeronautical engineer during the interwar years); they had more to prove as washed-up, exmilitary aviators (Tinker, Baumler, and Dahl); they were chronologically on the cusp of significant technological innovations in aircraft design and the formulation of more advanced combat tactics; and they served during the onset of the downward spiral of Republican Spain's military fortunes, and therefore were more acutely aware of the dire consequences of a possible fascist victory.

These men flew against primarily Spanish Nationalist and Italian aviators during their tours in Spain. Given their lack of sufficient flying experience, it is remarkable that most of them survived the air war at all, much less succeeded as combat pilots. The same can be said of the Spanish Nationalist and Italian airmen, a few of whom, with limited combat exposure in the Moroccan and Ethiopian campaigns, rose to the challenge through sheer flying ability and determination. As the competition stiffened, Tinker more than held his own against the well-trained German volunteers of the Condor Legion and their state-of-the-art aircraft.

Consideration of the groups as a whole suggests that there were enough malcontents and misfits to go around. The Acosta group caused themselves and their fellow mercenaries no end of trouble on both sides of the Atlantic Ocean. The tumultuous relationship between the November flyers and the Loyalist Air Ministry grew to international proportions when the airmen were expelled from Spain after government charges of alcoholism and nonperformance of duties. The outlandish attempt by Acosta to seize a Loyalist merchant ship in lieu of the Republic's alleged nonpayment of wages due him spotlighted an already growing controversy surrounding U.S. volunteers in Spain. Adding fuel to the debate were self-serving and self-laudatory media interviews, newspaper articles, and pulp magazine stories reported by the Acosta group which called into question the activities and objectives of comrades still fighting abroad.

The Whitey Dahl fiasco in Spain made headline news for thirty-two months, much to the chagrin of the Roosevelt administration and Congress. It came as no surprise, therefore, that from among the returning flyers one was chosen to pay for three years of bad press, and who better to assume that yoke than America's top scorer in that theater. While his former associates went on to fight other unofficial and official battles against fascism, Tinker was left to wither and die.

Aside from Tinker, the flyer Ben Leider represents perhaps the most tragic individual in this chronicle. Blinded by his hatred of all forms of privilege and entrenched plutocracy, of which he regarded fascism as the most virulent strain of all, he never considered for a moment his value to the Communists as a pawn. Unquestionably, Leider proved to be of more worth to Moscow as a dead martyr than as a live warrior.

If Leider served as the Escuadrilla de LaCalle's political commissar, social critic, and rabbinical counselor all rolled into one, Tinker's presence constituted the glue that held the squadron together. His folksy air and provincial background belied his cosmopolitan perspective, and his insouciant demeanor attracted the goodwill and support of both his Spanish and Russian allies. Following LaCalle's departure for the Soviet Union in the spring of 1937, Tinker's Spanish squadronmates demanded that he lead them in battle; shortly thereafter he was honored by the Soviets with an invitation to fly with them.

Of all the so-called mercenaries who flew in Spain for reasons already enumerated, only Fred Lord's remarkable career met the requirements. Assuming, therefore, that Tinker had experienced an ideological epiphany above the rooftops of Madrid on April 9, 1937, one might effectively argue that during his time in Spain he had never regarded himself as a mercenary. For this reason he perhaps felt at liberty to commit himself fully in the defense of a worthwhile cause. He doubtless perceived his generous remuneration to be nothing more than an incidental contractual deal for services rendered meant only to help him through a difficult time in his life. The fact that he gave no great moral weight to killing the enemy for profit in a just war may have otherwise confounded his friend Hemingway, who had seen in him an intriguing dualism of character when no such dichotomy actually existed.

For his compensation of $18,500, Tinker downed at least eight enemy fighter aircraft (as confirmed by his membership in the American Fighter Aces Association), and participated in the destruction of Nationalist bombers, anti-aircraft batteries, troop trains and convoys, railway depots, marshaling yards and ammunition dumps, munitions factories, and hundreds of fascist infantry in numerous strafing sorties. Whatever one chooses to call him, mercenary, altruist, or both, the adjective "unproductive" clearly does not fit this American. The Republic's investment in Frank Tinker paid handsome dividends over the course of seven action-packed months.

> [Cat Shannon] gave Jean-Baptiste Langarotti the £5000 remaining in his money belt from the operations budget, and the Corsican went back to Europe. . . . As he told Shannon when they parted on the shore, "It's not really the money. It was never for the money."
>
> Frederick Forsyth, *The Dogs of War*

Appendix A

THE MOST SUCCESSFUL REPUBLICAN FIGHTER PILOTS

Spain	Kills*
Andres Garcia de LaCalle	11
Manuel Aguirre Lopez	11
Miguel Zambudio Martinez	10
Manuel Zarauza Claver	10
Juan Comas Borras	10
Jose Bravo Fernandez	10
Emilio Ramirez Bravo	10
Felipe del Rio Crespo	7
Francisco Tarazona Toran	6
France	
Abel Guides	10-11
Rayneau	5
Laboussiere	5
Yugoslavia	
Bosco Petrovic	7
Russia	
Anatol Serov	13-16
Pavel Rychagov	15
Yeremenko	14
S. P. Denisov	13
V. I. Bobrov	13

Stepan Suprun	12-15
A. Lakeev	12
Ahmed Amba	8
Tarsov	6
Turshanski	6
<u>United States</u>	
Frank G. Tinker	8
Albert Baumler	4

*These figures are based on memoir literature as official sources are not available.

Appendix B

REPUBLICAN ARMS AND AIRCRAFT FROM ABROAD

From the beginning of hostilities, the Republicans sought to acquire arms and aircraft abroad and had encountered growing indifference from European banks, which either refused to accommodate their funds, on the pretext of complying with non-intervention, or purposely sabotaged their transactions. After Moscow underwrote the Spanish government, Loyalist Finance Minister Juan Negrin managed the transfer of the remaining gold reserve to Moscow from where it could be re-exported for arms purchases through Soviet banks. Negrin circumvented his cabinet in this negotiation under conditions of absolute secrecy. Of the $518,000,000 shipped to the USSR, around $333,000,000 did find its way back to Paris to pay for arms and combat aircraft. Concerned about the dedication of Stalin and his supporters to the cause, the Republicans continued to obtain arms, munitions, and planes from every available source through purchasing commissions established in Paris, Prague, and New York City. The balance of $185,000,000 the Soviets kept to pay for Russian material sent to Spain.

Appendix C

U.S. VOLUNTEERS AND THEIR CONTRACTS

Loyalist contracts with the American airmen became more competitive as time progressed and individual qualifications improved. Aviators Finick, Rosmarin, Lyons, Shapiro, and Leider signed on October 1, 1936, for $100 a week and 300 pesetas a month ($100 U.S. equaled 8 gold or 15 paper pesetas) with room and board under government auspices. With the exception of Semons, the entire Acosta group received $1,500 a month. Although a patriot and an effective recruiting agent for the Republic, Semons failed the basic flying requirements. On November 20 he agreed to serve as a gunner/bombardier with Grupo 15 at half the pay of his comrades. Chronic illness dogged him during the winter of 1936–37 and he had to be hospitalized in Paris where he would eventually liaise between Yankee pilots and the Air Ministry. Tinker's December flyers demanded $1,500 a month and a bonus of $1,000 for each enemy plane destroyed. Three of his messmates—Bell, Dickinson, and Gomez—suffered payment reductions due to mediocre flight tests, and two additional candidates were returned to the States.

Appendix D

REORGANIZATION AND INTEGRATION OF THE REPUBLICAN AIR FORCE

On May 19, 1937, Republican Spain was divided into eight Air Regions, replacing the former Escuadra system of organization: Madrid, Guadalajara, and Cuenca; Murcia, from Hellin to Almeria; Catalonia and eastern Aragon; Valencia, including Alicante; Ciudad Real, and parts of Estremadura; the Basque-Asturian enclave; Albacete and La Mancha; and Jaen and eastern Andalusia. The Air Regions corresponded to the construction and upkeep of more than 400 Soviet-built airfields in the Government zone during 1937, most being camouflaged rural homesteads, abandoned estates, or forests. Republican squadrons were later moved from field to field, often on a daily basis, to minimize the threat of surprise attack. The former Escuadra now represented an organizational entity, instead of a geographical unit, closely resembling the interwar "Commands" of the Royal Air Force.

There also occurred significant changes among Loyalist first-line combat pilots. A sprinkling of Spanish and American flyers joined Grupo 21's formerly all-Russian Mosca escuadrillas in the early summer of 1937; and the number of Spanish I-16 pilots dramatically rose thereafter. Among Grupo 26's four Chato squadrons, the Escuadrilla LaCalle was reformed with Spanish pilots and dispatched to the Basque zone, following LaCalle's departure to the USSR as head of the 2nd Promocin (training course). The 1st Chato Escuadrilla remained largely Russian until May 1938; the other I-15 escuadrillas being mainly or entirely Spanish from May 1937, onwards. The Government air war had become, little by little, a truly Spanish affair.

Appendix E

THE COMPUTATION OF AERIAL VICTORIES

During the Spanish Civil War, any aircraft forced to land outside its own airfield was classified as being shot down. Conversely the loss of an aircraft was admitted only if it had been destroyed. This formula explained the great disparity between claims, conceded losses by the enemy, and the payment of bonuses based upon spotty confirmations by multinational flyers. To confirm a "kill," one had to see the opponent catch fire, blow up, or hit the ground, or to see the pilot bail out. To follow a crippled adversary down was suicidal, as one became exposed to other enemy fighters in the vicinity.

Fortunately for Tinker and company, the Fiat CR 32's vulnerable point lay in its oil and water cooling systems as well as the location of the gas tank. The frontal positions of all three made the Italian fighter terribly exposed in a head-on attack. Red pilots always attacked from the front or below, and all Fiats lost burned in the air, thereby making confirmations easy. Unfortunately for Tinker, however, most enemy pilots learned to offer him as poor a frontal target as possible, displaying great knowledge and skill in aerobatics.

Appendix F

SYNOPSIS OF FRANK TINKER'S MILITARY TOUR IN SPAIN

From January 7 to July 29, 1937, the span of his combat tour in Spain, Frank Tinker flew a total of 191.20 hours and downed eight enemy fighters.

On March 20, Tinker piloted a Russian Polikarpov I-15 Chato pursuit (CA-056) out of Guadalajara. He destroyed one Fiat CR 32 during a two-hour flight and landed at Valencia. During a second mission that same day, he flew bomber escort and flamed a similar Italian fighter. While patrolling the Teruel front on April 17, in his Chato biplane pursuit (CA-058), he shot down a Condor Legion Heinkel He 51.

His next victories occurred after his assignment to the Soviet la Escuadrillas de Moscas (I-16s) commanded by Captain Ivan A. Lakeev. On June 2, Tinker dogfought with Fiats while flying bomber escort over Segovia. He bested a Fiat while flying an I-16 Number (CM-070). On June 16, he again destroyed a CR 32 in his Mosca fighter (CM-023). Scarcely a month later, on July 12, Tinker became the first American combat flyer to down a German Messerschmitt BF 109. He recorded his next "kill" five days later when he brought down a second Messerschmitt while on escort duty. Tinker notched his last victory the following day near Brunete (July 18) when he overcame a Fiat while escorting a squadron of R-5 Rasante bombers.

Appendix G

SYNOPSIS OF ALBERT J. BAUMLER'S MILITARY TOUR IN SPAIN

Albert J. "Ajax" Baumler recorded his first aerial "kill" with Kosokov's I-15 Russian squadron on March 16, 1937. In his Chato fighter (CA-023) on a sortie out of Soto Madrid, his patrol happened across a formation of Fiat CR 32s. The following dogfight occurred in the Brihuega-Valdesor-Pajares sector, and Baumler shared a victory with Soviet pilot A. N. Zeitsoff. Four days later, Baumler (CA-022) assailed a group of three Italian SM. 81 bombers escorted by five Fiat pursuits. Baumler destroyed a Fiat 10 kilometers southeast of Brihuega. On April 17 the American was on his second mission of the day, operating from a base near Sarrion, Teruel, when his group intercepted a formation of Heinkel He 51 pursuits. Giving chase to the enemy, Baumler crippled a Heinkel; as he did not see it crash, he was awarded with only a probable victory. The mercenary did, however, obtain credit for a subsequent "kill" in this same contest.

On May 30, Baumler and Frank Tinker were transferred to Polikarpov I-16 monoplanes. While flying his Mosca (CA-069) on June 2, Baumler flamed a Fiat over the San Idelrviso-Segovia area. Operating from Castejon on June 14, he brought down another Fiat over Huesca. Ajax's final victory occurred on July 8 in a Mosca (CA-022) out of Chozas Madrid. On this final sortie, he was escorting a formation of ten Rasante light bombers to Quejormas, when his group engaged an enemy force of bombers and fighter escorts. In the ensuing melee, Baumler downed a Fiat.

From December 27, 1936 to July 15, 1937, Baumler compiled 174.35 hours in service to the Spanish Republic. During this period, he was awarded three-and-a-half Fiats, one Heinkel He 51, and the probable destruction of a Fiat and a Heinkel.

SELECTED BIBLIOGRAPHY

For the convenience of the reader, I have avoided endnotes. Researchers will have noted that the historical framework of this story has come from the asterisked (*) memoirs in the following compilation of works consulted. The selected contents of these, sources penned by Spanish Republican and Nationalist pilots, U.S. flyers, and an English aviator, have been interwoven to present a concise and coherent narrative of the events leading up to the Spanish Civil War, with special emphasis on the unofficial U.S. air intervention in that conflict. Every attempt has been made to weed out historical error or personal exaggeration in a chronicle that by its very nature is largely devoid of "official" documentation. Of course, secondary sources have been used as a means of avoiding these historical pitfalls and to set the military events within a proper context.

BOOKS AND PAMPHLETS

Adams, Franklin P., ed. *The Collected Stories of Dorothy Parker*. New York: The Modern Library, 1942.

Angelucci, Enzo, and Paolo Matricardi. *Complete Book of World War II Combat Aircraft 1933–1945*. New York: Military Press, 1988.

Ardman, Harvey. *Normandie: Her Life and Times*. New York: FranklinWatts, 1985.

Baker, Carlos. *Ernest Hemingway: A Life Story*. New York: Charles Scribner's Sons, 1969.

Ben Leider Memorial Fund. *Ben Leider: American Hero*. New York: Ben Leider Memorial Fund, 1938.

Boyd, Alexander. *The Soviet Air Force: Since 1918*. New York: Stein and Day Publishers, 1977.

Brandt, Joe, ed. *Black Americans in the Spanish People's War Against Fascism,*

1936–1939. New York: Volunteers of the Abraham Lincoln Battalion.

Brome, Vincent. *The International Brigades, Spain 1936–1939*. New York: William Morrow, 1966.

Brown, David, Kenneth Macksey, and Christopher Shores. *The Guinness History of Air Warfare*. Enfield: Guiness Superlatives Ltd., 1976.

Capellá, Angel. *Hemingway and the Hispanic World*. Ann Arbor: UMI Research Press, 1985.

Constable, Trevor J., and Raymond F. Toliver. *Fighter Aces of the U.S.A.* Fallbrook: Aero Publishers, Inc., 1979.

Cooper, Stephen. *The Politics of Ernest Hemingway*. Ann Arbor: UMI Research Press, 1987.

Cortada, James W., ed. *Historical Dictionary of the Spanish Civil War, 1936–1939.* Westport,Conn.: Greenwood Press, 1982.

Coverdale, John F. *Italian Intervention in the Spanish Civil War*. Princeton: Princeton University Press, 1975.

Cull, John G., and Richard E. Hardy. *Hemingway: A Psychological Portrait*. New York: Irvington Publishers, Inc., 1988.

Dahiya, Bhim S. *The Hero in Hemingway: A Study in Development.* Chandigarh (India): Bahri Publications, 1978.

Eby, Cecil. *Between the Bullet and the Lie: American Volunteers in the Spanish Civil War*. New York: Holt, Rinehart and Winston, 1969.

Elstob, Peter. *Condor Legion*. New York: Ballantine Books, Inc., 1973.

Franks, Norman. *Aircraft Versus Aircraft: The Illustrated Story of Fighter Pilot Combat Since 1914*. New York: Macmillan Publishing Company, 1986.

Galland, Adolf. *The First and the Last: The Rise and Fall of the German Fighter Forces, 1938–1945*. New York: Ballantine Books, 1968.

Geiser, Carl. *Prisoners of the Good Fight: The Spanish Civil War, 1936–1939*. Westport, Conn.: Laurence Hill & Company, 1986.

Hallion, Richard P. *Strike from the Sky: The History of Battlefield Air Attack, 1911–1945*. Washington, D.C.: Smithsonian Institution Press, 1989.

Hemingway, Ernest. *The Complete Short Stories of Ernest Hemingway*. The Finca Vigía Edition. New York: Charles Scribner's Sons, 1987.

Howson, Gerald. *Aircraft of the Spanish Civil War, 1936–1939*.Washington, D.C.: Smithsonian Institution Press, 1990.

Hoyt, Edwin P. *The Airmen: The Story of American Fliers in World War II*. New York: McGraw-Hill Publishing Company, 1990.

Hudson, James J. *In Clouds of Glory: American Airmen Who Flew With the British During the Great War*. Fayetteville: The University of Arkansas Press, 1990.

Jackson, Robert. *Fighter!: The Story of Air Combat, 1936–1945*. New York: St. Martin's Press, Inc., 1979.

Johnson, J. E. *The Story of Air Fighting*. London: Hutchinson, 1985.

Kinney, Arthur F. *Dorothy Parker*. Boston: Twayne Publishers, 1978.

Landis, Arthur H. *The Abraham Lincoln Brigade*. New York: The Citadel Press, 1967.

——. *Death in the Olive Groves: American Volunteers in the Spanish Civil*

War, 1936–1939. New York: Paragon House, 1989.
Lustiger, Arno. *Schalom Libertad!: Judenim Spanischen Bürgerkrieg*. Frankfurt am Main: Athenäum, 1989.
Mason, Herbert Molloy, Jr. *The Rise of the Luftwaffe*. New York: Ballantine Books, 1975.
McCombs, Don, and Fred L. Worth, eds. *World War II: Strange and Fascinating Facts*. New York: Greenwich House, 1983.
Mitcham, Samuel W., Jr. *Men of the Luftwaffe*. Novato, Calif.: Presidio Press, 1988.
Mora, Constancia de la. *In Place of Splendor: The Autobiography of a Spanish Woman*. New York: Harcourt, Brace and Company, 1939.
Payne, Robert. *A Portrait of André Malraux*. Englewood Cliffs, N.J.: Prentice-Hall, Inc., 1970.
Proctor, Raymond L. *Hitler's Luftwaffe in the Spanish Civil War*. Westport, Conn.: Greenwood Press, 1983.
Ries, Karl, and Hans Ring. *The Legion Condor*. Westchester: Schiffer Publishing, Ltd., 1982.
Robinson, Anthony, ed. *The Illustrated Encyclopedia of Aviation*. Vol. XVIII. New York: Marshall Cavendish, 1979.
Rosenstone, Robert A. *Crusade of the Left*. New York: Pegasus Press, 1969.
Seagrave, Sterling. *Soldiers of Fortune*. Alexandria, Va.: Time-Life Books, 1981.
Thomas, Hugh. *The Spanish Civil War*. New York: Harper & Row, 1977.
Traina, Richard P. *American Diplomacy and the Spanish Civil War*. Bloomington: Indiana University Press, 1968.
Wyden, Peter. *The Passionate War: The Narrative History of the Spanish Civil War, 1936–1939*. New York: Simon and Schuster, 1983.

PUBLISHED AND UNPUBLISHED MEMOIRS, PAPERS, SPEECHES, AND LETTERS

Acier, Marcel, ed. *From Spanish Trenches: Recent Letters From Spain*. New York: Modern Age Books, 1937.
Baker, Carlos, ed. *Ernest Hemingway: Selected Letters, 1917–1961*. New York: Charles Scribner's Sons, 1981.
Bessie, Alvah, and Albert Prago. *Our Fight: Writings by Veterans of the Abraham Lincoln Brigade*. New York: Monthly Review Press, 1987.
*García LaCalle, Andrés. *Mitos y verdades*. Mexico: Ediciones Oasis, 1974.
*García Morato, Joaquín. *Guerra en el aire*. Madrid: Editora Nacional, 1940.
*Larios, José. *Combat Over Spain: Memoirs of a Nationalist Fighter Pilot, 1936–1939*. New York: The Macmillan Company, 1966.
*Peck, James L. H. *Armies With Wings*. New York: Dodd, Mead & Company, 1942.
*Salas Larrazabal, Jesus. *Air War Over Spain*. London: Ian Allan Ltd., 1969.
*Tinker, Frank G. *Some Still Live*. New York: Funk & Wagnalls Company, 1938.

*de Wet, Olof. *The Patrol Is Ended.* New York: Doubleday, Doran & Company, 1938.

PRIMARY ARTICLES AND PERIODICALS

"American War Birds in Spain." *Current History* XLV, no. 4 (January 1937): 107–108.

"Attack Orders: André Malraux Seeks Aid for Loyal Air Corps." *The Literary Digest* CXXIII (April 3, 1937): 15–16.

*Bell, Orrin Dwight. "I Fly in the Spanish War." *Liberty* XIV (December 18, and 25, 1937); (January 1, 1938): 6–11, 15–17; 37–39.

*——. "I've Stopped Killing for Money." *American Magazine* CXXV (June 1938): 35, 82, 84.

"Bertram Blanchard Acosta" and "Charles D. Koch." *Who's Who in American Aeronautics*, 3d ed., pp. 1, 66. New York: Aviation Publishing Corporation, 1928.

"Bruno's Last Flight." *Time* XXXVIII (August 18, 1941): 16.

"Bruno Mussolini." *The New Statesman and Nation* XIV (October 23, 1937): 639.

*Dickinson, Derek D. "My Air Duel with Bruno Mussolini" *Reader's Digest* XXXIV (March 1939): 34–37.

Dos Passos, John. "Room and Bath at the Hotel Florida," *Esquire* IX (January 1938): 35, 131–132, 134.

Dupree, F. W. "André Malraux" *Partisan Review* IV, no. 4 (March 1938): 24–35.

"Edith Dahl." *Variety Obituaries*, vol. 10, 1984–1986. New York: Garland Publishing, Inc., 1988.

*Finick, Eugene. "Bombers Aloft" *True Magazine* 15, no. 27 (August 1939): 75–93.

*——. "I Fly For Spain." *Harper's* CLXXVI (January 1938): 138-148.

Garnet, David, rev. "Some Still Live" *The New Statesman and Nation* 52 (October 29, 1938): 690.

Hawthorne, James. "American Fliers in Spain" *New Masses* XXIII (June 8, 1937): 17–18.

"Il Duce's Son." *Newsweek* XVIII (August 18, 1941): 28.

"Last Letters From Spain (Ben Leider)." *Current History* (April 1937): 46.

*Lord, Fred I. "The Education of an Adventurer." *New Masses* XXIV (August 10, 1937): 3–5.

*——. "I Faced Death in Spanish Skies" *Flying Aces* (June 1937): 7–10, 75–77; (July 1937); 8-10, 75–76.

"Lucky Among Moors (Harold Dahl)." *Time* XXX (August 2, 1937): 19.

McKenney, Ruth. "In Memoriam, Ben Leider." *New Masses* XXII (March 16, 1937): 6.

——. "Ben Leider: In Memoriam" *New Masses* XXX (March 21, 1939).

*Peck, James L. H. "Dogfight—A Lifetime in Forty Minutes," *The New York*

Times Magazine (May 26, 1940): 4.

*——. "Flying in the Spanish Air Force." *The Sportsman Pilot* IXX (February 15, 1938): 10–11, 31–32.

"Salamanca Saga (Harold Dahl)." *Time* XXXIII (April 10, 1939): 20.

"Soldier of Misfortune (Harold Dahl)." *Time* LXVII, no. 9 (February 27, 1956): 41.

*Tinker, Frank G. "I Fought in Spain." *Popular Aviation* (September 1938): 10–12, 82.

*——. "Some Still Live." *The Saturday Evening Post* CCX, no. 41 (April 9, 1938): 5–7, 74–80, 82; (April 16, 1938:) 1–16, 86, 88, 93–94; (April 23, 1938): 16–17, 55, 58, 61–62; (April 30, 1938): 18–19, 31, 33–34, 36.

SECONDARY ARTICLES

Carroll. George. "Wildest of the Early Birds (Bert Acosta)." *American Mercury* LXXXI (September 1955): 14–18.

Foxworth, Thomas G. "Bertram B. Acosta, 1895–1954." *Historical Aviation Album*, All American Series (1969 and 1970): 51–56, 108–112.

Herr, Allen. "American Pilots in the Spanish Civil War." *American Aviation Historical Society Journal* XXII, no. 3 (Fall 1977): 162–178.

——. "American Pilots in the Spanish Civil War: Addenda." *American Aviation Historical Society Journal* XXIII, no. 3 (Fall 1978): 234–235.

——. "On the Edge of Greatness: The Aviation Career of Charles D. Koch." *American Aviation Historical Society Journal* XXX, no. 3 (Fall 1985): 218–234.

McIntyre, Edison. "The Abraham Lincoln Battalion: American Volunteers Defend the Spanish Republic." *American History,* no. 1 (March 1983): 30–39.

Mizrahi, Joe. "The Phantom Brigade." *Wings* II, no. 2 (April 1972): 20–43.

Newton, Wesley Phillips. "Bertram Blanchard Acosta." *Dictionary of American Biography*, Supplement Five, 1951–1955, pp. 2-3. New York: Charles Scribner's Sons.

Prago, Albert. "Jews in the International Brigades." *Jewish Currents* XXXIII, nos. 2-3 (February-March 1979): 15–21, 6–9, 24–27.

Proctor, Raymond. "They Flew From Pollensa Bay." *Aerospace Historian* XXIV, no. 4 (Winter/December 1977): 196–202.

"Regia Aeronautica." Philip V. Cannistraro, ed. *Historical Dictionary of Fascist Italy* pp. 8–9. Westport, Conn.: Greenwood Press, 1982.

Richardson, R. Dan. "The Development of Airpower Concepts and Air Combat Techniques in the Spanish Civil War." *Air Power History* XL, no. 1 (Spring 1993): 13–21.

Rosenstone, Robert A. "The Men of the Abraham Lincoln Battalion." *The Journal of American History* LIV, no. 2 (September 1967): 327–338.

Scarborough, Bill. "Whitey Dahl's Luck Couldn't Last." *Climax: Exciting Stories for Men* (October 1957): 26–33.

Smith, Richard K. "Rebel of '33." *Shipmate* (March 1977): 31–34.

Wagner, Ray. "The Planes They Flew in Spain." *American Aviation Historical Society Journal* (Fall 1977): 179–180.

Watson, William Braasch. "Joris Ivens and the Communists: Bringing Hemingway Into the Spanish Civil War." *The Hemingway Review* X, no. 1 (Fall 1990): 2–18.

Winegarten, Renee. "The Reputation of André Malraux." *The American Scholar* LXI (Spring 1992): 267–274.

Wohl, Robert. "Republic of the Air." *The Wilson Quarterly* XVII, no. 2 (Spring 1993): 107–117.

OFFICIAL RECORDS AND PUBLICATIONS

United States. *Documents on German Foreign Policy, 1918–1945.* Series D (1937–1945), vol. III. Washington, D.C.: Government Printing Office, 1950.

United States. *Foreign Relations of the United States : Diplomatic Papers, 1937*, vol. I. Washington, D.C.: Government Printing Office, 1954.

G-2 Report from Townsend Griffis, Assistant Military Attaché for Air in Valencia, October 6, 1936. War Department Records, No. 2093-215, National Archives.

Report to G-2 from Assistant Military Attaché for Air Townsend Griffis, February 28, 1937. War Department Records, No. 2093-215, National Archives.

Contract List for U.S. Volunteers Flying for the Republic, February 28, 1937. War Department Records, No. 2093-215, National Archives.

U.S. Consul George M. Graves to Secretary of State, July 29, 1937. War Department Records, No. 2093-215, National Archives.

Communication from Secretary of War to Secretary of State, July 29, 1937. War Department Records, No. 2093-215, National Archives.

Communication from Assistant Attaché for Air Townsend Griffis, to State Department, August 2, 1937. War Department Records, No. 2093-215, National Archives.

G-2 Summary, August 3, 1937, War Department Records, No. 2093-215, National Archives.

Report to G-2 from Colonel Stephen Fuqua, Military Attaché, Valencia, February 16, 1938. War Department Records, No. 2093-215, National Archives.

War Department Interview with Derek Dickinson, September 1, 1939. War Department Records, No. 2093-215, National Archives.

Capture and Detention of Vincent Patriarca, November 13, 1936, Department of State Records, No. 8522221, National Archives.

Communication from Townsend Griffis, Assistant Military Attaché for Air, to the U.S. State Department. Department of State Records, August 2, 1937, National Archives.

UNPUBLISHED MANUSCRIPTS

Beck, Clarence D. "A Study of German Involvement in Spain 1936–1939." Ph.D. diss., University of New Mexico, 1972.

Drum, General Karl. "The German Luftwaffe in the Spanish Civil War." Unpublished manuscript, USAF, Air University, Maxwell AFB, Montgomery, Alabama, 1957.

Horton, Albert G. "Germany and the Spanish Civil War, 1936–1939." Ph.D. diss., Columbia University, 1966.

NEWSPAPERS AND JOURNALS

Atlanta *Constitution*, 1936–39.
Boston *Daily Globe*, 1936–39.
Chicago *Tribune*, 1936–39.
New York *Herald Tribune*, 1936–39.
New York *Post*, 1936–39.
New York Times, 1936–39.
PM, 1936–39.
St. Louis *Post-Dispatch*, 1936–39.

INDEX

Abraham Lincoln Battalion: organization; composition; size; action during the winter of 1936–37, 21–22, 77

Acosta, Bertram Blanchard, 24; aerial career; assigned to Sondica Airfield near Bilbao; flys Potez 54s and Breguet bombers in "Suicide Patrol"; refused bonus money; attempted defection and capture; cashiered from Loyalist airforce; return to U.S.; attempts to have Republican ship seized in lieu of lost wages and bonuses, 28–31; tormented life after return to America; lingers in tuberculosis sanitarium prior to death, 108–109

Aircraft, French Breguet (19) trainer/bomber, 7; Tinker escorts at Guadalajara, 67; Dewoitine (372) fighter, 12; Nieuport (52) fighter, 6, 18; Potez (540) bomber, 12

Aircraft, German Dornier (Do 17) "Flying Pencil, " armed recon./bomber, 48; Heinkel (He 45) reconnaissance, 16; Heinkel (He 70) reconnaissance, 16; Heinkel (He 51) fighter, 14, 16; first machines to arrive in Spain, 17; flee dogfight over the Jarama sector (seven machines lost in contest), 56–57, 73–77; Heinkel (He 59) floatplanes, 16; Junker (Ju 52) transport/bomber, 14, 16, 48–49, 51, 54–55, 68, 80, 97

Aircraft, Italian Fiat (CR32 fighter, 14; 16; Fiat (G 50) fighter, 110–111; Romeo (Ro 37) reconnaissance/lt. bomber, 16, 51, 87; Savoia-Marchetti (SM) S.81 bomber, 13–14, 16

Aircraft, Russian Polikarpov (I-15) fighter, 1; arrive in Spain and debut over Madrid, 14–15; performance and description of Russian pursuit, 34–35; Polikarpov (I-16) fighter: Americans are mesmerized by the sight of the Soviet Mosca (monoplane fighter), 37–38; Polikarpov (R-5) reconnaissance/lt.

bomber/ground-attack aircraft, 15, 67–68, 87, 89; Tupolev (SB-2) medium bomber, 67, 73
Aircraft, United States: Consolidated-Vultee (B-24) bomber, 109; Curtiss (F9C) Sparrowhawk fighter: Italian fighter pilots mistake Russian I-15s for, 15; Grumman (FF1) fighter, 109
Air Force (Spanish Nationalist): establishment of, 16–17
Air Pyrenees, 12
Airfields (Spanish) Alcalá de Henares (air base near Madrid), 27, 50, 55, 92, 97, 111; Alcantarilla (near Murcia): American flyers receive their Chato fighters at this base, 35; Campo Real, 95; Camposoto: situated on the estate of the Duke of Albuquerque and camouflaged from the air, 83–84, 92; Campo X (near village of Azuqueca): description of airfield, 44; diversions, 59, 92; Carmoli, 14; Guadalajara: description of base; Soviet and U.S. aviators stationed at field, 37–39; Lamiaco: Soviet fighter aerodrome near Bilbao, 29; Los Alcazares, 3, 14; San Javier, 6
Algora, 69
Allende, Javier, 74
Allison, James William Marion (Tex): ex-U.S. naval pilot from Dallas leaves pregnant wife to fly in Spain, 6, 24 assigned to the Escuadrilla de Chatos, 31, 37; petitions LaCalle for pilots' sidearms; discusses his past flying experiences, 39; downs adversary and is himself disabled in February 18th air battle, 53; recovers from wound received in air battle, 55; suffers from infected leg wound; threatened with amputation and flees to U.S. hospital; leaves for America in March, 1937, 59–60
Almadrones, 69
Almadrones-Brihuega highway, 65
Army of Africa: revolt in Spanish Morocco and poised to cross to Spanish mainland, 11; airlifted from Spanish Morocco to mainland, 14
Arnold, Gen. Henry H. (HAP), 108
Automotive Committee for Air Defense (ACAD): Koch serves as groups' technical advisor, 109
Aviators (German): Luftwaffe pilots debut in combat, 17
Aviazione Legionaria: strength of Italian air arm in Spain, 16; Tinker's contempt for Italian air force, 96; transfers all aircraft and equipment to Nationalists and embarks for Genoa, 105
Azaña, President Manuel: resignation, 105

Barajas, 91
Basques: side with the Republic, 11
Baumler, Albert J. (Ajax): December arrival who washed out of U.S. Army Air Corps training program, 6, 24; assigned to Russian Chato fighter squadron, 31; proceeds through qualification tests in Nieuport 52 and I-15 fighters; arrives at Los-Alcazares on heels of LaCalle Squadron's departure for Alcantarilla; renews old friendship with Koch; action on the Málaga front, 41–42, 57; transferred with Tinker to

Russian squadron at CampoSoto airfield, 83; first non-Russian aviator to be allowed to fly the I-16 Mosca, 86; visits E. Finick in hospital, 88; bags a Fiat in June 14th dogfight, 89; manages leave to Valencia, 90; July 4th celebration at Los Alcazares hotel with Tinker and Dahl, 91; downs Fiat in Villa de Cañada sector; strafes fascist trenches at Casa de Campo, 92; hospitalized with throat infection and leaves Spain for U.S., 95; returns to U.S. via Canada, 100; attends New York University; assists Tinker in lawsuit brought by O.D. Bell; goes to China and flys briefly with Chennault's AVG outfit; later joins USAFF in 1942 as officer pilot; serves in Korea as GCA controller, 109–111

Bell, Orrin Dwight: early military career and business failure, 5, 24–25; returns to U.S., 71; sues Tinker over *Some Still Live* articles in *SEP*; assisted by former squadronmate Derek Dickinson; suit dropped and resurrected after Tinker's death; joins U.S. Army Ferry Command in 1943; passes away the same year, 110–111

Bercial, Luis, 56

Berenson, Bernard, 80

Bermudez de Castro, Narcisco, 21, 51

Bernard, Rep. John T.(Minnesota), 107

du Berrier, Hilaire, 24

Berry, Gordon, 24; assigned to Sondica Airfield; flys in Suicide Patrol; attempted defection and capture; released from Loyalist air force, 29–31

Bicycle pilots: General Queipo de Llano's derisive term for Republican airmen (radio), 50

Bilbao: Basque capital taken by Nationalists, 90

Blanch, Lt. Antonio: death of LaCalle's third patrol leader, 65

Blue Patrol, 21, 51, 54

Blum, Premier Leon (France): sends consignment of aircraft to Spain, 12

Boddem, Feldwebel Peter: downs Whitey Dahl during July 12th dogfight, 93

Bolshevik, 14

Brenner, Samuel, 24; alone remains with Anglo-American Breguet International Squadron, 31

Brihuega, 50, 62, 64, 67, 69

Brihuega-Guadalajara highway, 65

Byrd, Commander Richard E., 29, 109

Calderon, José, 43

Caldwell, Nord, 24

Calle de Alcalá, 81

Calvo, 73; 76

Campaigns Aragon: Republican Spain divided by Franco's armies, 101; Brunete: Republican offensive; Loyalist military objectives; Rebel occupation of Brunete; Franco redeploys troops to bolster Madrid front; Government drive checked and Nationalist counter-attack; stalemate begins again; Condor Legion participates, 91–92 Catalonian: Nineteen Rebel divisions face twenty weakened Red divisions; German ME109s dominate the skies; Morato's 3-G-3 Group downs nine Government

bombers, of which Morato claims three; As de Bastos and La Cucaracha Italian Groups claim 24 Loyalist machines, 104 Ebro: Republican aims; commencement of the Loyalist offensive; Rebel forces halt drive and initiate own offensive, 102–103
Canary Islands, 11
Carney, William, 94
Casa de Campo, 1
Cascon Briega, Manuel, 29
Castenedo, Chato, 37
Cerro de los Angeles, 50
Chamorro, 44; 47
Chennault, Gen. Claire, 106
Columbia *Missourian*, 25
Comas Borrás, Juan, 74
Condor Legion: formation of, standing size of compliment, 16, 91; leaves Spain at wars' end, 105
Cot, Aviation Minister Pierre, 12
CTV (Corpo Truppi Voluntarii), 16, 69

Dahl, Edith Rogers: entertainer, 4; resides in Cannes, 5; petitions Franco for Whitey's life; remains in Cannes; continues to perform in Parisian nightclubs during husband's imprisonment; welcomes Dahl home and leaves him at dock; goes to Australia; dies at eighty-one, 112–114
Dahl, Harold Evans (Whitey): loses commission in Army Air Corps, 4; contracts to fly for Republican Spain; arrested and released; marries Edith Rogers, 5; assigned to Escuadrilla de Chatos, 31, 37; blond hair and florid complexion fascinates Spanish squadronmates, 39; shot down in Feburary 18th contest, 53; unharmed in February 18th contest; gives account of his activities after downing, 55; "liberates" artifacts from estate home, 59; on furlough in Madrid; meets writer Ernest Hemingway, 60; flys reconnaissance at Guadalajara, 62, 68; receives medical furlough and leaves for Paris; returns to squadron amidst controversy, 71–72; reassigned to Spanish Chato outfit, 71–72; July 4th celebration at Los Alcazares hotel with Tinker and Baumler ; stationed with Spanish Chato squadron at CampoSoto during Brunete fight; goes down in July 12th dogfight; parachutes and lands among Moorish troops; nearly killed by captors; taken to headquarters and ultimately Salamanca where he is incarcerated; international incident develops; suggest U.S. is pro-Republican; later recants innuendos, 91–94; trial date set by Rebels; found guilty and sentenced to death on October 8th (1938); Edith Dahl requests Franco to grant clemency; Dahl languishes in prison; court sentence overturned by Franco; Dahl spends remainder of war in Salamanca prison; released on February 22, 1940 and returns to U.S.; breaks up with Edith; leaves for Canada and commission in the Royal Canadian Air Force; remarries; cashiered by RCAF for selling non-surplus equipment; flys for Swissair; allegedly steals gold buillion bar from cargo hold and is fired; imprisoned and awaits trial; free on bond and

leaves for Canada; flys supplies to Arctic radar sites; killed in crash on February 14, 1956, 112–114
Debs, Eugene V., 25
Dequal, Capt. Vincenzo ("Limonesi"): arrives to command first Fiat squadron, 18
Dickinson, Derek, 24; qualifies as observation pilot and assigned to Barcelona, 71

Earl Carroll's *Vanities*, 4
Eberhard, Oblt. Kraft, 17
Escuadre España, 6; uses Barajas airport as base; fighter escorts led by Abel Guídes; action; replacements; decline; reformed into Escadre Malraux and Málaga campaign, 12–13
Escuadrilla de LaCalle: created at Los Alcazares airfield; formation of "La Patrulla Americana"; experience of its members, 33–34; flyers embarrass LaCalle before townspeople of Albacete; Tinker, Dahl and Allison redeem LaCalle's honor; ordered to Guadalajara; near fatal accident involving Leider and Chato Castenedo during flight to destination, 36–37; combat debut over Jarama River; bomb and strafe gunpowder factories, 42; returns to Guadalajara airfield; bombs and strafes Rebel troop trains soon thereafter; guns become unsynchronized and destroy propeller of Tinker's ship; machine experiences vibrations with new propeller, 45–46; losses from February 18th air battle, 53–54; leads Loyalist counterattack on the Jarama front; strafes Nationalist artillery emplacements, 55; deputy squadron leader Luis Bercial lost in battle, 56; receives first replacement pilot at Campo X; "over-the-top" aviator worries Tinker, 61; aerial battle of March 14th, 65–67; LaCalle reorganizes during Guadalajara fight, 68; leisure time and pilot entertainment, 70–71; end of LaCalle's command, 72

Fagnani, Capt. Tarscisco, 21; commander of Fiat Group in Spain during Jarama struggle, 51; relieved of duty following Jarama campaign, 54
Faldella, Col. Emilio: Gen. Mario Roatta's chief-of-staff killed at Guadalajara, 63
Finick, Eugene, 24; early life; pilots Russian bombers and groundstrafers (R-5 Rasantes) on the central front, 27–28; vows revenge for Leider's death, 52; flys R-5 in final stage of Jarama campaign, 61; pilots Rasante against Italian columns, 67–68; goes down in R-5 during June 2 air battle; nearly killed by Republican militia; subsequent hospitalization and rotation back home, 88
For Men (magazine), 110
Franco y Bahamonde, Gen. Francisco, 10–11; England and France extend diplomatic relations to government, 104–105
Fredavore, 107
French government: support of Republic, 12

García, Justo, 68
García Gomez, Manuel: abandons

family and military career in Guatemala to fly for the Republic, 5, 24; assigned to the Escuadrilla de Chatos, 31, 64, 68–69; Tinker encounters in Valencia during layover prior to trip home; tells Arkansan about term as POW following his downing; swears to fly again, 99–100

García LaCalle, Andrés: commands the Escuadrilla de Chatos; hero of Talavera de la Reina with eleven victories, 31; physical description and demeanor, 34, 38, 46; version of Leider's death, 52, 54, 60–62; promoted to major and leaves for Russia; outline of subsequent military career; describes Dahl as more aggressive than Tinker in combat, but endowed with less judgment, 71–72, 77, 82, 109

García Morato y Castano, Joaquín, 16–17; prewar military career, 18; first combat sortie and victory; co-pilots Ju 52 bomber with Carlos Haya; bombs aerodrome at Cuatro Vientos; drops 250 kilogram bomb on the patio of the Loyalist War Ministry; joins Dequal group; leads patrol with Dequal and Montelli; records his fifteenth victory over Madrid; discord with Fagnani and creation of Blue Patrol, 19–21; ordered by Gen. Kindelán to the Jarama front, 51, 54; idol to fellow Fiat pilots, 71, 74; reforms squadrons 1-E-3 and 2-E-3 into Fiat Group 2-G-3; appointed commander of the new unit, 86–87, 96; brings down his fortieth victim near Iqualada on January 19, 1939, 104; perishes in accident at Seville air show (April 4, 1939); Franco awards title Count of Jarama, 105

García Pardo, Lt., 17

Garibaldi Battalion, 49, 63, 67

Gellhorn, Martha, 77–78, 82

Gijón, 101

Gorrell, Henry, 77

Graves, U.S. Consul George M., 94

Great Britain: refuses to entertain idea of assistance to Loyalist government; Non-Intervention Committee formed in London, 12

Great Depression, 2, 5

Gregoric, 95

Griffiss, Capt. Townsend: Asst. Military Attaché in Valencia is accused by Dahl with having pro-Republican leanings; grilled by War and State Departments, 94

Ground crewmen (Loyalist): numerous mechanics and armorers outrank the aviators they serve; LaCalle asks that mechanics eat and sleep separately from pilots, 44; squabble over left-wing politics; U.S. flyers settle the dispute, 47; reaction to losses of the American Patrol in February 18th dogfight, 53

Groups, Italian Fiat Group, 51, 54; As de Bastos (23rd Italian Fighter Group), formation and duty sector, 87; Collacicchi-Sforza's Romeo Ro37 Group, 69; Fagnani's Fiat Group, 69; La Cucaracha (16th Italian Fighter Group), formation and duty sector, 87; Raffaelli, Tenento Colonnello Ferdinando: bomber from his Savoia-Marchetti SM 81 Group downs Lieutenant Antonio Blanch; 65

Groups, Spanish Loyalist All-Spanish combat squadrons: Republican Air Ministry's objective, 33
Groups, Spanish Nationalist Fiat escuadrilla (all-Spanish): creation of I-E-3 following Jarama air battle, 54; Morato Group, 89; Heinkel Group 2-E-2: Salas' pilots acquit themselves well during course of the war, 77; Morato Groups (2-G-3) and (3-G-3): accounts for 151 Government machines destroyed; García Morato's tally at 34 victories in late July, 1938; destroys targets along the Ebro loop; new Group, 5-G-5, created in November; three Groups become the 7th Fighter Squadron with Morato as its Commander, 102–103
Guídes, Abel, 13
Guadalajara, Battle of: U.S. aviators involvement; threat of massive Italian infantry columns; wide-spread use of ground strafing by Loyalist aircraft; Red pursuits based near scene of battle; rains slow Italian advance against Madrid; repeated attacks on fascist armor and troops; Italian soldiers flee; enemy advance stalled; air battle of March 14th; Italian prisoners believe themselves fighting in Ethiopia, 61–70

Haile Selassie, 3
Hefter, Lt. Ekkehard, 17
Hemingway, Ernest: makes Dahl's acquaintance, 60, 77–82; praises Tinker's account of his Spanish tour in *The Saturday Evening Post*, 101; admits to having suicidal impulses; assesses Tinker as a Hemingway hero, 106
Herndon, Angelo, 107
Holland, Sydney, 30
Honess, Uffz. Guido, 93
Hotels: Ben McGhee (Little Rock), 105; Florida (Madrid), 77–81; Gran Via (Madrid), 92
Houwald, Hptm. Ottheinrich von, 17
Huesca, 88–90
Hull, Cordell, Secretary of State, 94

International brigaders: arrive in Spain, 15; on furlough in Madrid, 81

Jackson, "Baldy": fictional surrogate for Harold (Whitey) Dahl in *Night Before Battle*, 79
Jarama, Battle of : early Rebel attempts to take Madrid, 50–51; climax of struggle, 61
Jeréz de la Frontera, 14
Jiménez Bruguet, Alonso: succeeds LaCalle as squadron commander, 72

Kantz, Walter, 6
Kindelán, Gen. Alfredo: chief of the Nationalist Air Force, 16–17; wants Spanish pursuit units equipped with Fiats, 51, 54
Kishinev massacre, 25
Klein, Lt. Alfons, 17
Knuppel, Hptm. Herwig, 17
Koch, Charles D. (December arrival): oldest U.S. volunteer flyer in Spain; background; graduates as fighter pilot in Spain, 6, 24; assigned to the Escuadrilla de Chatos, 31; leads "La Patrulla Americana", 34; suffers from ulcerated stomach; cannot make move to Alcantarilla

and is replaced by Chang Selles; never rejoins the LaCalle Squadron, 35; flys with Baumler on the Málaga front; U.S. pilots are part of an I-15 squadron commanded by a Russian named Kosokov; Koch's first "kill", 41; notches second victory in Jarama campaign; fights alongside LaCalle squadron; four sorties with Kosokov squadron on Feburary 18th, 54; 57; flys Chato at Guadalajara; suffers stomach hemorrhage and is separated from service; 68; returns to U.S. and resumes profession as an aeronautical engineer; retirement and death on September 5, 1983, 109–110
Kopets, Ivan, 69
Kosokov, 54, 69

La Granja, 87
Lakeev, Commander Ivan A., 72; squadron assigned to Barbastro, 88
La Patrulla Americana: flyers get better acquainted at Guadalajara base, 39–40, 49–50
Le Havre, 3
Leider, Benjamin David: early life and newspaper career; serves as transport pilot during early stint in Spain, 24–27; assigned to the Escuadrilla de Chatos, 31; moral compass of the American Patrol, 34, 39; claims Heinkel He 51 in air battle, 46; killed in air battle of February 18th, 51–53; return of body to U.S.; fanfare orchestrated by the American Communist Party; memorial services at Carnegie Hall; laid to rest in Flushing, New York, 107–108
Leider, William, 108
Lerroux, Alejandro, 10
Lewis, Joe E., 4
Liuzzi, Commander Alberta: killed during Guadalajara battle, 63
Lord, Frederick Ives: invites Koch to fly in Spain as Republican volunteer, 6, 24–25; assigned to Sondica Airfield; early WWI flying record; nearly shot; flys in "Suicide Patrol"; attempted defection and capture; released from service, 29–31
Los Rios, Fernando de, Ambassador, 12
Lufbery Circle, 51
Lukács, Gen. Matazalka Kemeny: killed by Morato, 89
Lyons, Edwin, 24; pilots transports and Soviet Rasante light bombers/ground strafers, 27

Madrid: Rebel army threatens existence, 1–2; Nationalist revolt fails, 4; fascist daylight bombing ceases, 15
Madrid Corps, 50
Madrid-Saragossa highway, 62
Madrileños, 1, 81
Magic Fire (Operation), 16
Magriña, Rafael, 68, 77
Malraux, André, 6; participation in civil war; offers volunteer flyers lucrative contracts; makes film *Sierra de Teruel*, 12–13; U.S. tour; returns to Spain and attends the second International Congress of Writers in Madrid, 57–58
Manzanares River, 1, 50
Mar Cantábrico, 31
Marqués del Merito: defends Dahl in Rebel court, 112
Marty, André: commandant of the

IBs in Spain, 22
Matthews, Herbert, 77–78
Mercenaries (U.S. Aerial): hard life; author's definition, III-VII; arrival of September, November, and December groups; methods of recruitment by U.S. Communist and Socialist parties; Republican Spain's requirements of aerial volunteers, 24–25; food, mealtime routine, exotic delicacies, and dietary problems, 40–41
Mexique, 4
Modesto, Col. Juan: Negrín places crumbling Loyalist army under control of pro-Communist officer, 105
Mola, Gen. Emilio: captures most of northern Spain, 11
Monte Garabitas (Casa de Campo), 81
Moors: cruelty of African soldiers was legend; Loyalist pilots attempt to conduct aerial battles over friendly territory, 39
Mora, Constancia de la , 52
Moreau, Capt. Baron Rudolph von, 18
Moroccan War of 1909–1926, 11
Mussolini, Bruno, 110–111

Navalpotro, 69
Negrín, Dr. Juan: assumes control of Republican government in its last days, 105
New York *Post*: Leider employed as "flying reporter, " 26
Night Before Battle: fictionally chronicles an evening with Hemingway and U.S. flyers at the Hotel Florida, 79–80
Nobili, Capt. Guido, 51, 56
Non-Intervention Agreement: inked by most European capitals and U.S., 12
Normandie, 3, 4, 6
North American Newspaper Alliance, 78
Noville, George, 109

Operazioni Militari Spagna (OMS), 16

Palmero, Lt. Jaime, 73, 76
Paramount Theater (Madrid), 82
Pascual, Lt. Ramiro, 16–17
Patriarca, Vincent: draws his native U.S. into an international incident, 19; repatriated, but returns to Italy and enlists in Regia Aeronautica; migrates back to Spain and again flys for the Insurgents; survives the war and serves in North Africa during World War II; ends career in Naples at U.S. naval base, 111
Pavlov, Gen. Dimitri: commands Red armour units at Guadalajara, 63
Plotkin, Rev. Benjamin, 108
Port Bou, 3–4, 100

Queipo de Llano y Serra, Gen. Gonzalo, 11, 50

Rambaud, Capt. Luis, 16
Raye, Martha, 4
Reader's Digest, 110
Rinehard, Howard, 6
Roatta, Gen. Mario, 62–63
Roosevelt, President Franklin D.: early attitude toward U.S. IBs in Spain, 22
Rosmarin, Joseph, 24; transport pilot, 27
Rosmarin, Pauline: serves as interpreter for Col. Yacob

Schmonskievich, 27
Russian Villa, 90

Salamanca, 93–94
Salas Larrazábal, Angel: military background; desires to join the Dequal Group, 19–21; leads 2-E-2 Heinkel Group in April 17th air battle, 73–74, 89
Salvador Diaz Benjumea, Lt. Julio, 16–17; military career; enlists in Dequal Group, 19–21, 51; assumes leadership of Morato's old squadron, 87
San Francisco, 2
San Sebastian Pursuit Squadron: forerunner of German Condor Legion, 30
Santander, 101
Sanz Sainz, Augustin, Sub-Secretary of Air , 24–25, 110–111
Saturday Evening Post, 101, 110
Schacter, Samuel (New York City attorney): go-between in U.S. for Republican Spain pertaining to matters of recruitment, 24
Scheele, Major Alexander von, 14
Schmidt, Vincent Minor, 24; transports fighters from France to Spain; survives Spanish Civil War to command the 14th Volunteer (bombardment) Squadron in China in 1938; flys in International Squadron in Finland (1939–40), 111–112
Schmonskievich, Col. Yakob: takes command of Soviet air operations, 15
Schneider, Edward, 24; assigned to Sondica Airfield; flys in "Suicide Patrol"; attempted flight and capture; released by Air Ministry, 28–31
Segnaire, Julien, 13
Segovia, 87
Selles, Chang, 39; background on girlfriend Christina, a seamstress at Campo X, 45, 59; on furlough in Madrid, 60–61, 65; false report of his arrest and execution as a Japanese agent, 86
Semons, Edwin, 24–25; serves as recruiter and liaison officer for the Republican Air Ministry, 28, 94
Seville, 14
Shapiro, Arthur, 24, 26; flys Soviet SB-2 medium bomber in early raids on the Alcázar fortress in Toledo, 27
Sierra de Teruel, 13
Sierra Guadarrama: crest marked boundary between Government and Rebel territory, 38–39
Some Still Live, 96, 101–102
Spain, Republic of, V; collapse of government on March 29, 1939, 104–105
Spanish Civil War, IV; background and outbreak, 9–11; early stages, 11–12; intervenes in conflict, Germany, 13–14; intervenes in conflict, Italy, 13–14
Sperrle, Gen. Hugo: commander of German Condor Legion; holds rank equivalent to air theater commander, 16
Stalin, Premier Joseph: reasons for Stalin's intervention in Spain; a Soviet presence, 14
State Department, United States, 15, 103

Tablada (Seville): aerodrome and depot seized by Insurgents, 11
Talavera de la Reina, Battle, 17
Tarzan: German Shepherd mascot of LaCalle Squadron, 71

Teruel: air battle of April 17th, 73–77
Thaelmann Battalion (11th IB): decimated in Jarama struggle, 50
Tinker, Frank Glasgow, Jr., xii; experiences epiphany over Madrid, 1–2; birth; parents; adolescence; graduation from Annapolis ('33); enlistment in Army Air Corps; training at Pensacola air station, 2; assigned to cruiser *San Francisco*; commission dissolved; tries to volunteer for Ethiopian air force; seeks contract to fly in civil war Spain; alias, Francisco Gomez Trejo; signs contract; reports to Loyalist Air Ministry in Valencia; reports to Los Alcazares airfield, 3; reports to Breguet 19 bomber squadron at Manises Airfield with Koch and Dahl, 6–7; brief stint in Breguet International Squadron, 24; assigned to the Escuadrilla de Chatos, 31, 35–36, 40–41; attacks Rebel artillery on February 11 sortie; witnesses explosion of left wingman's I-15; strafes fascist troops at secondary target; offers condolences to dead flyer's comrades, 42–43; Campo X; own mechanic outranks him; living quarters; background on girlfriend, Maria, a seamstress at Campo X, 44–45, 46–47, 48–49; believed Italian pilots to be cowards; conversely, shows great respect for German aviators, 49; air battle of February 18th, 51–54; diversions at Campo X, 59; Madrid, 60; attacks Italian columns at Guadalajara, 64; first victory, 66; records second kill, 68; base life, 70–71; does not succeed LaCalle as squadron commander, 72; reassigned to Teruel; replaces Alonso Jimenez as commander of LaCalle's old squadron (in the air), 73; air battle of April 17th, 73–77; Madrid, 77–82; transferred to Russian squadron at CampoSoto airfield, 83; strafes Rebel convoy on Madrid-Burgos highway, 84; leisure time at CampoSoto, 84–85; first non-Russian to fly the I-16, 86; learning to fly the Mosca, 86; fourth victory and a "probable" near Segovia, 87; visits Finick in hospital, 88; bags fifth enemy fighter in final air battle over Huesca, 89; stationed at Liria and Los Alcazares after fall of Bilbao, 90; wounded during furlough at Costa del Sol, 90–91; Brunete campaign, 91; records sixth kill against a Messerschmitt, 93; blames Air Ministry for Dahl's downing; leads Soviet squadron; number seven victory is another Messerschmitt; downs Fiat for eighth and final victory, 93–96; is persuaded to leave service, 97; long journey home; writes account of tour in Spain, 100–101; suicide, 105–106
Trautloft, Hptm. Hannes, 17
Trijueque, 63

Ukov, 88

Vallee, Rudy, 4
Velardi, Gen. Vincenzo: Commander-in-Chief of the Aviazione Legionaria during battle of Jarama; ordered airmen

not to overfly Red territory, 51
Villa de Cañada, 92

Warlimont, Lt. Col. Walter: replaces von Scheele as Hitler's commander in Spain and military advisor to Franco, 14
deWet, Olof, 37
Wise, Rabbi Stephen S., 107

About the Author

JOHN CARVER EDWARDS is a Special Projects Archivist at the University of Georgia. He has authored dozens of historical articles and two books, *Patriots in Pinstripe: Men of the National Security League* (1981) and *Berlin Calling: American Broadcasters in Service to the Third Reich* (Praeger, 1991).